STUDIES IN IDEALISM

STUDIES
IN
IDEALISM

BY

HUGH I'ANSON FAUSSET

KENNIKAT PRESS, INC.   PORT WASHINGTON, N. Y.

STUDIES IN IDEALISM

First Published in 1923
Reissued by Kennikat Press in 1965
Manufactured in U.S.A. by Arno Press, Inc.

Library of Congress Catalog Card No: 65-18603

TO

LASCELLES ABERCROMBIE

IN GRATEFUL ADMIRATION

OF HIS GENIUS

AND this our life, this admixture of labour and of warm experience in the flesh, all the time it is steaming up to the changeless brilliance above, the light of the everlasting snows. This is the eternal issue.

D. H. LAWRENCE, *Twilight in Italy.*

PREFACE

IT is often argued that any attempt to explain poetry in terms of reason is doomed to failure, that it can neither help anyone to write poetry nor, for that matter, to enjoy it. There is truth in the assertion. A poet gives living form to abstractions, he images life and philosophy. Yet only by a rational interpretation of the spiritual values of life can we test the truth of his insight or the value of his experience.

Criticism may not lead anyone to poetry, but it may refine the pleasure of those who are already wed to her, or help the diffident to approach her with discretion. For men are first drawn to poetry by instinct. Poetry interprets life emotionally, and save with natures of a rare and precocious refinement, men are at first attracted by its most physical expressions, be they sensuous or sentimental, irrespective of their triviality. Yet it is to such men, strongly responsive as they are to emotion, that poetry can most powerfully speak. And as mind is latent in all matter, as form is potential in chaos, so in uncritical instinct resides the energy out of which the vital vision of the seer may take shape. One of the functions of criticism should be, then, to help men to sublimate their emotions,

to differentiate in poetry between the expression of
accidental sensation or personal appetite and that
which is rendered real and absolute by its rational
content, so that we can say of it that it has the
permanence of truth as well as the allurement of
beauty. For the truest poetry is an experience of life
realised in imagery and, partially at least, disintegrated into thought, as distinct from a slavish
imitation of life or a chain of thoughts suffused by
feeling. An essential emotion can then be distin-
guished from an accidental, not only by the extent
to which it moves us, but by the vital vision, the
innate philosophy, which its expression disintegrates,
and which is susceptible of analysis. True poetry
embodies a profound apprehension of life: it relates
particular experience to a body of past experience,
subconsciously criticised, to the rhythm of universal
nature, to the morality of human reason, so that the
experiences of such a poet, though particular, are
never trivial. For they are one with the life-principle,
with that primary creative emotion in which all
thought is contained. Even the momentary emotions of such men are portentous. For into the
smallest measure of time and of space they intrude
a sense of the infinite and the eternal. The experience, however, of the lesser poet is particular to
himself, either because his emotion or his reason is
too weak to liberate him. He does not realise life
intimately from within, nor project himself into

conditions of life other than his own, and the meanness of his thought is often balanced by the vagueness
of his feeling. He sees life as an alien spectator and
imposes his own fancies upon her phenomena,
borrowing her images arbitrarily, and fitting them
together artificially to give the illusion of life or
illustrate his own logic or sentiment. His poetry is
a trickery of manner lacking organic necessity.

All experience, therefore, teaches us that there are
degrees of reality, and the greatest poetry is that
which approaches the highest and purest degree of
consciousness. The great artist widens man's comprehension, and sharpens his apprehension of life by
expressing it with a new intensity of experience and
from a new aspect. The poet has certainly suffered
much at the hands of the pedant who tries to relate
his world of vision to a scheme of logic, and he may
perhaps be justified in crying, " I feel and so I
know," and bidding us feel too and say no more about
it. Yet in his own interest there are two arguments to
be urged against this. In the first place, the content
of the sublimest poetry is generally beyond the un-
educated faculties of men. All great art of an enduring
quality strikes even the initiated at first as somewhat
austere: to the sentimentalist its life is so immeasurably purer than his undeveloped sense of values that
it seems to be dead. There is scarcely a superlatively
great poem in the world to which mankind was
emotionally true enough to respond immediately.

And secondly, to put the emotion of the poet beyond
the range of criticism is to encourage the charlatan
far more than the genius, and to invite men to confuse
the two. For how are we to test the value of an emotion
save by reference to rational values? The affectation
of a self-conscious versifier, the violence of a physical
realist, the soaring spirituality of a Shelley—each has
its perfect right to expression. But we were fools not
to discriminate between them, and estimate their
worth in the light of thought as well as of sensation.

For true vitality is the only quality which criticism
is justified in demanding of a poem. To inquire
whether a poem is moral, graceful or alluring is
usually to confuse the issue. We should ask rather
of every work of art, " Do we find here, beneath
however cultivated an exterior, only death and
sterility, or is this an organism charged with intense,
creative and harmonious life? Is it the offspring of
deep and ardent feeling, of a sensibility generously
responsive to life, and of a critical insight able to
disentangle the significant from the irrelevant, or
is it born of a destructive or dilapidated egoism,
incapable of any but self-centred emotions, or apt
only to exercise its wit and cleverness upon the
surface of existence? In short, is it vivid expression
or calculated self-indulgence? The term " art "
has constantly been used to cover ineptitudes of
expression which if perpetrated in action would
merit contempt from men of true sincerity. For

the truth is that art undefined may be as mean and
adulterated, as false and feeble as life, it may be
even more dead to consciousness than life at its
worst can be. " Art for life's sake, and life for art's,"
is the only justifiable banner for a poet to carry.
For the beautiful is the real—physically, intellectually, morally and spiritually, and a true poem is
the most finely poised and the most intensely vital
organism of which we can conceive.

Some critics, however, would attempt to distinguish the true value of a poem from the purely
artistic, the external standpoint. They would examine the style, and were they master artists they
would probably discover the values aright. For
in true poetry form and matter are one, and their
relationship must be inevitable, so that in the
grace and intensity of the style, or its languor or
artificiality, we should be able to judge the value
and truth of the emotion. But it is a dangerous
method, and many critics who base their judgment
on technical analysis are engaged without knowing
it in little more than a post-mortem examination.
In fact, like the artists whom they are seeking to
criticise, they come to value style for style's sake
instead of for what it expresses. Often a poem may
in form appear to be a living organism; it is well
manufactured, but without spiritual validity. And
the difference between the necessity of art and the
ingenuity of artifice is not always easy to detect.

But the critic who tries to pierce beyond and through
the form to the idea, to the degree of spirituality,
of philosophy, of experience, contained in the poem,
though he may not consciously analyse the concrete
graces of form, such as the intricacy of image or
the prosodical cunning, is at least likely to discover
whether the poem is really a living organism and
what degree of consciousness it embodies.   In art
it is just as bad to sacrifice flesh to spirit as spirit
to flesh, to concentrate exclusively on either the
style or the matter.   The perfect poem is that in
which the purest and most universal experience of
life is embodied in the richest and most particular
form, and so closely must the two coincide, so
exactly must the matter answer to the spirit, that
we are conscious only of that sense of enlarged
and rarefied reality which we name beauty.   Much
poetry scarcely touches upon this reality, much
touches it only for moments and then with adulteration.   In these studies I have attempted to define
what that reality is, and how man's realisation of
it has grown more pure and profound, particularly
in his poetry, as he has become more conscious
of rational values. No definition of absolute life is
possible.   Poets can convey the essence of it by
creating life anew nearer to their desire for beauty
and their vision of truth, philosophers can tabulate
some of its principles.   I have tried here to combine
the methods of both, because I hold that true

morality no more in art than in life is a matter of
fancy, but represents the conclusions of inspired
reason, and that a failure to distinguish the ideal of
the sensualist, under whatever disguises, from that
of the seer and the saint and the poet in their
sublimest expression explains almost all the evil
that has come upon the world.

In the ideal development of literature the advent
of Christianity is the first great landmark; with this
I have dealt briefly in one chapter. In that of our
own poetry two periods of renaissance, adolescence
or of awakening to new vision, are manifest—the
Elizabethan age and the Romantic revival with
which the eighteenth century ended and the nineteenth century began. Between these lies a period
of apparent artificiality, of selfish wit and artistic
cunning, which, however, served to bridge the gulf
between the uncritical surrender to natural beauty
which the age of Marlowe and his successors represents and the pursuit in and through and beyond
nature of a beauty in which intellectual and human
values were more and more championed, always
with zeal and often with indiscretion. In this second
idealistic and humanitarian period Wordsworth,
Shelley and Keats are each in English literature
particularly significant forces. Of Keats I have
already written elsewhere [1]; Shelley's conception
of life I have reserved for a separate study. In the

[1] See *Keats. A Study in Development* (Martin Secker).

following studies I have been compelled often and dangerously to generalise, to seize upon the salient features of large periods as mirrored in the writings of some of their most expressive characters, rather than examine minutely the practice of individuals, which may to some extent, though I think only superficially, seem to challenge in particulars my general assumptions.

Moreover, I have considered here both poetry and life from an absolute standpoint, so that readers may be moved to protest at times with Hamlet, "How absolute the knave is!" In an age which is devoting itself with such success to relative analysis and a study of the particular, it may seem rash to attempt once more a universal synthesis. Yet some such re-statement seems the more necessary because idealism has become rather discredited through some element of falsehood in men's conception of it, which has led to error and to a disappointment only the more grievous for the high hopes which men were once invited to entertain. The time, indeed, is ripe to rescue "Idealism" from that pursuit of the pleasing abstract, that cultivation of the vaguely high and fantastic, that blindness to actuality and indulgence in narcotic dreams to which it was reduced in the last century, particularly by German "Romantic" culture. Men in their revolt from the celestially detached concepts of Hegelian philosophy and bloodless formulas of

beauty and virtue, have tended to deny " Idealism "
categorically. The more, therefore, is it necessary
to distinguish " Idealism " in its truth from the
" Sentimentalism " which usurped its name; to
distinguish, in fact, visionary reality (the offspring
of imagination) from creations of fancy and lies of
plausible instinct; to relate once more man's desire
for perfection, where it has degenerated into a desire
for self-gratification, with actuality; to reconcile intellectual and natural values. Victorian idealism has
taught us that " necessity " cannot be shirked
without a loss both of physical and spiritual health.
The natural can neither be forgotten nor suppressed,
however " ideal " or " refined " a man may deem
himself to be. It must be faced, analysed, understood and so mastered, not by denial, but by a re-
direction of energy to comprehended ends. The true
idealist, in fact, as distinct from the fanatic, not only
visions men as potentially perfect, but observes them
as they are. And so, neither being obsessed by
egotism nor the slave to abstractions, he does not
end by desiring like Robespierre to guillotine every
one for failing to fit into his system. Between a too
hasty idea of perfection, however, and an unenter-
prising acceptance of things as they are, the western
world has for many centuries preserved an imperfect
equilibrium. In turn the materialist has crucified
the idealist, and the idealist has sown the seeds of
disruption in the conventional order of the materialist;

and so only at the cost of excess and destruction, of exaggerated rebellion and bigoted resistance, has the life principle been able to advance towards a higher expression of itself in the matter of man. For lack of purity of motive and understanding on the part of the idealist, and through the gross insensitiveness of the materialist, no orderly evolution from a physical to an ideal conception of life has been possible. Yet for the first time perhaps in the history of mankind there are signs of a more general sensitiveness to the reasonable and the humanitarian, and a denial of a physical dispensation. In the development of man we may trace three stages: the first animal, in which he is the slave of instinct; the second imperfectly conscious, as he is led through pain, the consequence of instinctive licence, to study his conditions and control his energies, where reason and experience tell him that a surrender to them will entail suffering; the third a sublimation of instinct into idealism, when he has become sufficiently conscious and disinterested to pass beyond selfish calculation and welcome life once again as a sensation to be enjoyed, but as one so refined and spiritualised by reason that it is purged of all the dangerous destructiveness of the physical. Man thus advances from the instinctive to the partially conscious, and thence to a higher form of instinct, altruistic and spiritual, in which all consciousness is merged. He grows out of matter until he is conscious of his particularity, and through self-criticism and analysis of his conditions he at last escapes the particular and realises life completely by putting himself into harmony with his fellows and the universe. Self-consciousness is thus the disease through which men must pass to spiritual health or pure consciousness.

In his poetry we see this development at times completed where in the actual life of to-day it is but just begun. Yet the two are distinct provinces only in the sense that absolute poetry is a condition of existence to which life must always tend and may in some far day attain. Literature, no more than life, as some suppose, is a pastime: it is rather a field of battle where the soul strives with the body, and in its moments of high triumph is reconciled with it. In life this reconcilement must be long delayed. That absolute equality, that enthusiastic liberty, for example, which has been the watchword of every revolutionary creed, can only prove admirable and even attainable when the nature of all mankind is evolved and educated up to the point of using and not abusing such a condition. But towards such a condition it is the duty of all true and selfless men to strive, ever on guard against that compromise with the forces of self-interest and obscurantism of which the churches have too often been the sad example.

In these studies, then, I have attempted to keep

B

consistently before me the light of that desirable
ideal, and I have therefore judged men and periods
great in so far as they reveal the " will to know "
and the " will to be " active in their endeavours, in
so far as I see them surmounting difficulties and
ever straining onwards to a higher conception of
their being and a fuller realisation of life.   My
subject has thus compelled me to pursue always the
counsels of perfection, but I am not blind to the
merits of the less good because they cannot compare with the merits of the best, to talent and
accomplishment   ruling   their   smaller   kingdom
because superlative genius sets out to embrace the
universe.   I would repeat one word of apology.   It
may be argued, as I have said, that in attempting to
explain rationally the miracle of imagination I have
undertaken an impossible task.

Poetry in its absolute moments passes utterly
beyond ratiocination.   It transcends logic as the
spiritual transcends the physical and the intellectual.
It reveals life eternally, and the instruments of time
are too mean to record its mystery.   Metaphysics
are as inadequate as physics to capture the essence
of that ecstasy.

Such pleading is in a sense unanswerable: and
my aim in these studies has not been to rationalise
the mystery of great poetry, but to prove that its
reason, if immeasurably higher than logic, is yet
based on truth and not on fantasy.   Creative beauty
and truth, particularly after their confusion in the

Victorian Age, need relating. In the highest moments
of poetry they are one, revealing to us the purest
consummation of life: but short of the highest
their union is imperfect, and either element may
debase the other.

I have tried here only to illustrate, so far as
reason can, the principles which distinguish the true
heirs of imagination from the bastard offspring of
sensationalism, sentimentalism and affectation, and
to trace in a general way the degree of creative
consciousness to be found in English poetry at
different periods and at different moments in the
career of individual genius. I have tried, in short,
to resolve once more what Plato has called " the
ancient quarrel between poetry and philosophy."

Where, then, I have used the term " Reason," it
must be understood to denote something very
different from the conscious intellect, and by
" Philosophy " I do not mean any systematic
phantom of the schools. Many critics will deny
that a poet has a philosophy, because his philosophy
is something different from that of Aristotle or
Kant or Dr. Bradley. His philosophy is an intuition
or a series of intuitions concerning the universe.
These certainly he does not build up logically into a
system. For a system or a formula is of necessity
removed from that fluctuating life with which a
poet must directly commune. Behind the poet's
senses that absorb, profusely and unconsciously,
behind his reason that sifts and defines experience,

but is sterile in itself, must be the life-force, the
spiritual energy, which, blending the two together
in a perfect instrument, creates through them a
new reality. But if he is to be more than a trifler
in the craft of pleasure, if he is to serve truth as
well as life, a poet must, however unconsciously,
evolve from his impressions a synthesis, a profound
attitude towards life which colours all his experience
and gives tone to his lightest expression. The degree
of a poet's imaginative intensity corresponds exactly
with the extent and subtlety of this synthesis, realised
unconsciously doubtless in the moment of poetical
expression, but gradually formed by the action of
his critical reason upon the matter of instinct. By
the quality of his synthesis alone can we estimate a
poet's stature and permanence.

It is true that few poets have consciously
rationalised their intuitions: their reasoning is
implicit in the action of imagination as distinct
from that of fancy. Yet in the passive periods
which must intervene between those of creative
effort, a poet may well examine his intuitions and
criticise his vision of life in sober prose. It is because
the criticism of poets has been based on creative
experience that it has generally been of such value,
and we believe that increasingly, as the rational
era into which we have been born advances, poets
will be found submitting their emotions to analysis,
not for the purpose of discrediting feeling, but of
deepening it. Such a process is evident in the letters

and private memoranda of more than one great modern poet.

At the same time the critic, in trying to assess the truth and value of experiences which poetry images, or in tracing the advance of genius from fancy or affectation to imaginative power, is as bound to use some of the broad definitions of philosophy as he is to consult the data of modern psychology. Certainly, except for those happy few whose intrinsic taste can be relied upon to distinguish the tones of imagination from those of fancy, unreal ornament from living form, ecstasy and insight from pleasure and charm, some degree of philosophical reasoning must enter into the serious critic's method of exposition.

To reflect upon life and upon oneself, and so to master both and direct them aright, I take to be the tendency most generally significant of progress in our era. The modern world, in its very perversities and crudities, has begun consciously to substitute Reason for Necessity, and to assert higher values than the physical. Reason, which always, if we look carefully enough, will be found irradiating unconsciously and imperfectly the darkness of primitive genius, though for long submerged in the physical, has become, for the artist of our own time in candid daylight, the "headstone of the corner." Reason must ever draw upon instinct for inspiration and experience; for unless it has its roots in Nature it must wither up and die, as for example it did in the eighteenth century. But it yields itself no longer blindly to the forces of Nature. It has learnt to rebel as a prelude to learning to discriminate. It will go to Nature for the sublime, but it will not surrender its dignity to her wantonness.

The hope of the future of that civilisation which seems sometimes to totter so dangerously near the abyss is that the inspired Reason, the sympathetic Imagination revealed by the true poet, artist or seer, may yet emerge from and impose itself upon the new inventiveness, the self-interested mental cunning of which the last century witnessed so marvellous a development. For it is this enlightened Reason, and not any negative and dogmatic moral code, which alone can prevent the creative energy of the life-force from degenerating, as it so invariably has done throughout the history of the western world, into a fatal destructiveness. It must be our aim, as Renan wrote half a century ago, " to correct and better creation," not to surrender blindly to a life-force which lacks all fine discretion save on a physical plane. The Gothic structure of the old world in all its grandeur and disproportion has fallen in ruins about us. Our efforts must be directed towards the conscious construction of a surer and better-balanced edifice, in which all humanity may live at peace and realise their differing geniuses in a common harmony.

In the straining of individual genius after deeper truth, no less than in the history of literature sur-

veyed broadly in its progressive fluctuations, we
see the soul of man feeling out towards this purer
and more harmonious ideal of life. And in the
following essays it is upon this aspect alone that
I have fastened, rejecting, often against my will,
more particular and alluring prospects. In short,
I have viewed certain epochs of poetry for the light
they throw upon the growth of the human mind,
emerging gradually as the directing power among the
faculties. To some it may seem that poetry should
not be made to serve such dreary purposes, or beauty
be dragged at the chariot wheel of truth. Yet I can
conceive no higher service for either poetry or man
to pay than that of asserting and guarding humanity's
prerogative. The beauty of the natural world survives only in that of the spiritual; without truth
art degenerates quickly into an idle entertainment
or a cultivated affectation. In so saying I have no
desire to enforce a barren Absolute, to imprison
within a system and methodise Nature's infinite
variety, to drain life of colour in a passion to have it
clean. Embracing our faith in Reason must be a
passionate devotion to human nature, to life itself
and its transcending of a rational mechanism by
creative beauty. Life without reason degenerates
into luxury, waste and effeminacy: reason without
life into impoverished dogma. The one is the sin
of Naturalism, the other of Puritanism. A passive
acceptance of life must be balanced by an active
direction of it. The masculine and feminine principles

must blend in the joy of vital equilibrium. Thence only can spring beauty, ordered but electric, an art of life that is both urgent and at peace. As in social ideals the true aim must always be to achieve a world in which there is enough system to prevent waste without encroaching upon liberty, in which there is justice, but not the justice of the automaton, so in æsthetic ideals we must beware of fettering the potentialities of life, we must welcome the interaction of the forces of the ideal and real, of the aspiring and the acquiescent upon which the vitality of art depends, and through which it rises to those entranced moments when the dualism is resolved and in a perfect reconciliation of elements we touch the heart of the eternal mystery.

But the pain of the world has in recent years unfitted many of us for the enjoyment of minor graces and elegant pleasures. Our manhood protests that we should take our small part in trying to lessen that pain for the future. Reason in its amplest exercise alone can do that service, and as science can conquer physical pain, and philosophy mental, so poetry, rightly conceived, can triumph over the agony of spiritual sickness and admit mankind to the absolute liberty, to the radiant health of life lived according to love.

H. I'A. F.

Newtown, Newbury.

CONTENTS

STUDIES IN IDEALISM

CHAPTER I

THE RELIGION OF POETRY

> Our life is but a little holding, lent
> To do a mighty labour; we are one
> With heaven and the stars when it is spent
> To serve God's aim: else die we with the sun.
>
> G. MEREDITH, *Vittoria*.

I

No personality impresses the modern mind with
more significance than Goethe's: all the groping
energies of past ages, all the passions of primitive
man, find their consummation in him. But they
are accepted, enjoyed and analysed by the same personality. The same genius that responded ardently
to the errant stimuli of life, turned in its quieter
moments to question and accuse. The scientific
mind had come to trouble the artist's self-absorption.
Yet in Goethe the two paths of approach to life rarely,
if ever, met, and it is this failure of coincidence that
left on his career the stamp of disproportion, of
gigantic imperfection. He could not rationalise a
passion till the passion had had its way with him:
emotion and reason strove together within him,

1

the victory tending now to the one, now to the other, and the issue remained for ever inconclusive. Yet we cannot regret an irreconcilement which we owe to the very force of genius. Goethe's temperament was intolerant of rational control in the moments of its activity, but in the periods of revulsion which must accompany a powerful pursuit of sensation we enjoy the rare spectacle of a detached philosopher and psychologist analysing situations which he himself has experienced. We profit as much by the intimacy as by the extent of experience which his restless craving for sensation, his instinctive delight in the obscure and violent depths of life, guarantee. In the same person we witness the limited mind of the scientist examining the limitless passions of the artist. " Often," he wrote, " I appear to myself like a magic oyster over which strange waters flow." In sober retrospect the genius of a colossal sentimentalist dissects itself, the fever patient becomes his own doctor. This self-observant analysis is essentially modern.

The twentieth century intelligence has learnt to distrust any blind surrender to instinct, whether its manifestation be physical or ideal. It no longer accepts intuitions as unimpeachable, it refers them to the reasoning faculty. For the imagination which seeks to take truth by storm may well find itself in the citadel of error.

It is our hope to demonstrate that all great art

is the result of inspired reasoning; that the ideal
world of the poet is no phantom of dreamy sentiment, but only a more concrete embodiment of the
most enlightened philosophy and the most searching science; that although, as Plato declares, he who
would share the enchantment of the Muses must seek
them in no sober-minded spirit, his intoxication is
such that it clears the mind instead of clouding it,
that it accelerates the mind's action by the potency
of nature, and enriches its substance with all the
inherited experience of man—that poetry, in short,
is the most positive, the most economic, the most
penetrating, the most communicative reading of
human life. Moreover, the distinctive quality of
poetry in the brotherhood of the arts is that it reveals life not more intensely, but more intelligibly,
than either music or painting. Not only by its
ecstasy can it captivate and convince the senses,
but by its definition it informs through them the
mind. Music, for example, by the infinite suggestion
of sound-waves compels an almost complete surrender
of the other faculties to the sense of hearing. Its
elemental power is far beyond that of poetry. But
poetry, even in its highest moments of exaltation,
when sound and sense are magically merged,
interprets experience with a subtlety and an
exactness to which all the faculties can and should
respond. Moreover, its medium of language is
the distinctive creation of humanity and is alone

capable of embodying the finest gradations of human values.

If, therefore, absolute poetry may be proved to combine in itself all avenues to truth, to satisfy the requirements of philosophy in its inspired wisdom, of religion in its realisation of the beautiful and the good and its essential portrayal of ugliness and evil, of science in its creative analysis of human motive, of humanity in the fervour and depth of its sensibility, of nature in the emotional pulse of its rhythm, may we not with justice name it the consummation of all man's most pure and disinterested desire? may we not consider it the highest of all faiths, " out-topping knowledge " because it embraces it all? may we not, if we can prove to our reason that its merits are such as we claim, see it as the inevitable inspiration of that world it foreshadows, in which beauty is the only morality and love the only law?

Such expectations may well be Utopian, and it were foolish to indulge them. Yet a critic of the arts to-day who is at all responsive to the conscience of his age or to the signs which foretell the outlook of to-morrow must realise that if he is to strengthen the appeal of poetry he must determine first to explain its mystery. He must humble himself to interpret its ecstasy to the logical mind.

The critic and the artist, like the priest, have enveloped their activities too long in the veils of superstition. Art, which is the most universal of all languages, which breaks down all conventional barriers and scorns all greedy prejudice, has been for three centuries at least the sanctuary of a few initiates. It may be argued that the purity of its utterance cannot capture the hearing of normal men. But we answer that all hearings are insensitive until they are educated, and we see in our own day hosts of new unjaded minds to whom poetry spells revelation and a clear vision of life if an informer will but tell them how to look and where to set their eyes. If we consider reason in its widest implication as the first principle in the morality of the modern world, we must demonstrate the sanity of great art, we must show that passions allied to reason can teach man to live as felicitously as, uncontrolled by reason, they can hurry him to his ruin; we must prove to him that the guiding principles which produce a great poem will, if applied to the life of man, guarantee an existence joyous, ample and free, and that, until man has accepted the laws of art as the standard of his habitual conduct, he may enjoy a foretaste of that ultimate harmony in the great poetry which is his heritage.

Beauty, in short, needs definition. It is because art, unlike philosophy, appeals to man's mind through his senses that it has shared the disregard which practical intelligences allot to every form of emotionalism. But true art is more reasonable than logic, and more moral than religion. Its function is not merely to soothe the nerves or feed the senses or drug the conscience. It is not a luxury or a hobby or an agreeable decoration to life, but a model of life lived fully and without prejudice to others or discord amid its elements. And only those who approach art prepared to endure the same struggles which the artist himself underwent in searching the darkness for light and resolving the discords into harmony can taste the ecstasy of perfect living.

It is for the critic then to differentiate the phenomena by which Beauty expresses herself, to reveal the laws to which the poet submits, to translate into the language of the mind truths which are expressed in the language of the heart. Only thus can he hope to convince men of the reality of poetry and of its correspondence with the practical concerns of life. Only thus can he combat the tendency of provincial minds to reduce art to an eclectic craft, pursued for its own ends, to oppose it to morals, to divorce it from humanity, to exaggerate its mystery, to exploit its manner at the expense of its matter.

2

The world, we feel, has reached a transitional point, and the conflict between the acceptance of traditional faiths and their rationalisation is everywhere evident. The ingenuous return to nature with which the last century began has been largely discredited. It has been found to have represented less a return to Paradise than a plausible reversion to barbarism. The equilibrium of nature was disturbed at the Renaissance by the first serious intrusion of self-consciousness upon animal instinct, and for more than two centuries and a half in Western Europe instinct and intellect have been engaged in inconclusive and increasingly embittered warfare. The problem before the modern world is to reconcile them. Certainly we have found the spontaneous *laissez-faire* of organic impulses, championed in the early nineteenth century, to be inapplicable to a world of human values. Such a hasty and instinctive optimism has resulted in a cruel waste and brought a vast catastrophe. Art, which is sensitive to every change in human consciousness, has not been slow to record this. Everywhere we realise, if we study the symptoms, that we have lost the spontaneity of generations who were willing and glad to observe beauty in life or nature externally, we have put by in distrust that unreasoning faith, that appreciative fervour which inspired men to express life with careless, impulsive munificence. Circumstances have forced on us a loss of faith and a growth of self-consciousness. The condition we believe to be temporary, but if we are ever to regain that credulous childhood out of which all art in augmented waves

c

of consciousness has flowed, we shall do it, not by
an emotional reaction, but by a rational advance.
We shall regain our belief in life, and so our love
of it, without which no art can be born, by learning
to understand and direct it, and then with a faith
enriched by reason we shall know life to be an act
co-extensive only with consciousness itself. The
purging of instinct by reason and the enlargement
of thought by feeling represent the poet's consciousness. With him the critical and creative faculties
coincide, with men in general they customarily
alternate. Thus it happens that at present our
generation is more critical than creative.

We represent in fact but one more of those critical
reactions against uncritical creation which have
recurred throughout the ages. We see man in turn
surrendering himself to nature with undiscriminating
sympathy, only to draw back later aghast at the
cruelties and errors which such an abandonment of
controlling reason entails, to exaggerate then in
panic the rights of his determining ego. But in
turn his moral judgment becomes impoverished and
false, in so far as, out of timidity and an instinct
of self-preservation, he is divorced from a free experience of nature and her principles. And there
follows inevitably another revolt toward nature at
all costs. Yet in the critical reaction of our own day
we detect more liberal traits than, for example, in
the eighteenth century. We are not to-day emphasis-

ing the rights of intellect to the complete exclusion
of the wealth and impulse of nature. We are in fact
attempting from a critical standpoint a reconciliation
between human and natural values, between life and
reason; we are striving towards an ideal harmony—
tentatively, to be sure, because we are fearful of
licence, but with a more enlightened purpose than
ever perhaps in the history of the world. We see
this intention alive both in art and in social theory—
and we can associate its inauguration with no one
more fittingly than Goethe.

For Goethe was too vital to fear his passions—
he indulged them, and then criticised their quality:
in this how different from Rousseau, who indulged
his feelings in wild timidity, and sentimentalised
them in retrospect. The importance of Goethe is
that his nature felt the two claims of passion and of
logic, and that throughout his life we witness the
conflict of these two claims, the temporary triumph
now of one and now of the other, the final defeat of neither. To the survival of both we owe
his instructiveness. The problem which Goethe
attempted to solve, of explaining his intuitions of
life to his reasoning faculty, is that which faces
every critic of art and of life to-day. For if reason in
its widest implication is to prove the morality of the
world, that art only is likely to survive which is adequate to the reason as well as to the instinct of man.

We, who see in the life and art of the last century

so many examples of feeling indulged at the expense of thought, have not the courage to express our feelings until we have convinced ourselves of their honesty. Even Goethe experienced the halting difficulty of one who would test his feelings in the school of logic. Writing in old age, after a life spent in passionate experimenting, he confesses how impotent a man is when he attempts to translate a mere desire for perfection, however ardent, into a conscious creed upon which he may act.

" From religious feeling," he says, " no man will hold himself aloof; it is impossible for him, however, to contain his feelings within himself, and he therefore seeks or makes proselytes. The latter is not my way: the former I have faithfully tried to carry out, and from the creation of the world I have found no confession which I could have accepted in its entirety. Now I learn in my old age of a sect, the Hypsistarians, who, hemmed in by heathens, Jews and Christians, declared that they would treasure, admire and honour the best, the most perfect, that might come to their knowledge and, in so far as it might stand in near relation with the Godhead, pay it reverence. Then at once a cheerful light broke on me from a dark age, for I felt that all my life long I had been endeavouring to qualify myself for a Hypsistarian. That, however, costs no little effort, for how comes man, in the limitations of his individuality, to know what is more excellent? "

The true poet is always he who, hemmed in by heathens, Jews and Christians, seeks, not to formulate a creed, but to treasure, admire and honour the best, desiring both to re-create the world in the joy of its truth and in so doing to criticise the pain of its error. He is one who has, in Keats's memorable words:

> A power within him of enormous ken
> To see as a God sees, and take the depth
> Of things as nimbly as the outward eye
> Can size and shape pervade.

We may perhaps pause here for a moment and question with profit why conventional religion has so generally failed to meet the idealistic requirements of a poet. All gods, we must remember, represent in origin the idea of perfection common to the age which conceives them. They are the arbitrary creation in primitive times of man's instinct, in later days of both his instinct and his faulty intelligence. The religious conceptions of primitive men are identical with their poetical. Their gods were images of natural forces which the mind was too simple to understand, and which awoke, therefore, spontaneous emotions of fear and reverence. This sense of something vast and unintelligible in the world of nature led them to conceive their gods to be at first particular phenomena of nature, and later but larger versions of themselves. The gigantic stature corresponded to their frightened realisation of the infinite force of nature, the human configuration to the self-absorption of the savage mind which had no means yet of escaping from its own limitations. These gods therefore reflected all the virtues, vices and appetites of savages: they took shape as the earth herself in the convulsions of natural law, and they are unmoral as nature, beautiful as the spring in all its urgent promise, terrible as the thunder.

As man's intelligence grew, however, and he began to reflect on his actions both in relation to himself and to others, he came to realise that some were prudent and led to immunity from danger, and others to personal disaster. At first he imputed such variations in occurrence to the malignity of his gods, revenging themselves for some failure of respect. Nemesis dogged his footsteps, and every casual lapse of reason on his part was imputed to the punitive instinct of the goddess. The mind of man was still but a fitful taper flickering helplessly in the midst of a great darkness. Through the gradual experience of ages he learnt, however, his capacity, limited though it was, to act with discretion. The idea of free-will was born, and its province has widened with every century. Religion reflects this discovery in its increasing recognition of man's distinctive moral responsibility. The various figures in whom men associated their later ideas of perfection were no longer mere symbols of organic energy, or of tyrannical law, although such a seer as Mohammed still included in his religious system purely savage beliefs and practices. Christ alone of these later reflections of the divine idea represents a perfection in which

the ultimate moral idea of love—of enlightened reason
—is untainted by any surrender to grosser appetites.
He is the image of all that poetry must seek to be:
but the tragedy of Christianity as an institutionalised
faith is that its master-figure has been overshadowed
by the primitive tribal deity, created by the Jews in
the infant period of their racial history, to represent
the conception of natural rather than rational law,
a being whom men in the ignorance of instinct
worshipped for its physical power, and to whom
they offered the reverence of dread. It was in the
spirit of this symbol that all those deeds have
been done in the name of Christianity which may
fitly be summarised in the phrase "the cruel mercy
of the cross."

Protestantism in its reaction from a corrupt
humanism exaggerated an error which scholarly
culture was beginning to remove: puritanism and
a church tied to an imperialistic state has perpetuated
it in England almost to this day. If we consider the
conception of God held by the general conscience
even of the last century, we shall find Him representing, if not the mere face of nature or the omnipo-
tent and often malignant ogre of primitive minds,
yet a vague, quixotic power which it was as useless
as it was disrespectful for man to attempt to analyse.
A knowledge of Him, men urged, could only be
attained by faith, by an intuitive surrender to the
unknown, to an experience in which individual

reason was forgotten in an identification of the whole being with a universal energy, too vast and too manifold for limited human intelligence to explain to itself. This cosmic power, conventionalised to suit the tamer needs of men, took the form of kingship, and of that less agreeable type of monarchy which the Greeks stigmatised as despot. That such a being should be responsible for an economic system which gave to some men a life of degradation and to others one of self-indulgent luxury seems in no way to have shocked the moral conscience of our grandfathers; so easily may instinct, unsupported by reason, impute to divine consecration a system for which only careless, and so criminal, irrationality is responsible.

Indeed the Victorian Age, in which a class religion, represented by the Church of England, commanded general respect and exercised wide influence, reveals the confusion of the primitive symbol and the unconsidered fact at its worst. We have shown how the god of a savage imagination was an enlarged fact of existence, an exaggerated being who combined in himself all that man feared and admired in nature and in the more powerful of his fellow-beings, and how this arbitrary creation partook of all the unmoral nature of fact, as it is accepted by instinct and yet unestimated by mind. Only by degrees has man come to discriminate between the attributes of power and of intelligence, and to demand that his God should symbolise not only cosmic energy but also human morality, that is, energy directed by sympathetic reason. The Victorian generation excused the failures of human intelligence which resulted in wars, pestilences or starvation, by referring them to a cosmic energy which admits none but physical values. They were fatalists because they were content with their own comfort in what was still essentially a primitive social system, and the method best calculated to perpetuate their good fortune was to proclaim a divine confirmation of it.

Further, the symbols by which primitive man conveyed the idea of the life-force, or their own battle-lust, or erotic emotions, appeal too directly to the immediate appetites to be discredited by anything but the wide education of men's reason, or by the awful warning of ruinous experiences clearly traceable to unregulated instincts. But just as we no longer deem the thunder to be an expression of our God's indignation, so we will come to view with incredulity a generation which could impute to the will of an omniscient and virtuous God a national war, an epidemic of typhoid, or a street accident. The development of religious belief presents, therefore, the spectacle of mankind gradually refining upon their idea of God, and bettering the symbol in which they have embodied that idea; gradually purifying it also of those facts of contemporary life which superstition has attached to the idea; in short, ceasing to

surrender their free-will to the symbol which they
themselves have set up. For having made gods in
their own momentary likeness, instinct has led them
invariably to impute to and excuse in these self-
created phantoms all the disabilities under which
they themselves suffer as a result of their own inadequate exercise of reason. But that gods were
humanly created by man's imperfect consciousness
not only of first causes but of perfection, was an
admission which superstition still refused to allow.
The forces of nature were still so deified that man
stood by and watched them working havoc in thou-
sands of lives with reverent acquiescence. For the
tradition of natural godhead, which had sprung from
man's incapacity to understand or control organic
forces, was so strong that human reason was in no
way outraged by all the evils which were imputed to
their god's agency, and which, we might have supposed, would have led them earlier to question his
omnipotence and omniscience.

The process, then, by which men make for themselves gods is in origin a poetic one. It is that of
imaging an idea. For the poet seeks to abstract
the reality from the phenomena about him and recreate it. But in doing this, unlike the priest who
constructs a temple about the poet's image, he is
possessed by as disinterested a passion as the scientist
examining matter under his microscope. He takes
joy in every expression of life, but because he loves

beauty he is eager to choose only such vital elements as form a harmony, and so reveal in their expression an innate and active principle of reason: but if he is compelled to represent energies warring together for lack of rational direction, he records their discord with an equally passionate fidelity to truth. Nor does he seek to persuade others to worship any of the experiences which he embodies, however perfect his own sensibility may deem them, to the exclusion of others, wherever they are to be found. He is the passionate spectator of life, with a preference for the pure and lovely life, because his emotions respond to harmony with an exquisite gladness, to discord with a sense of its denial or adulteration of creative reality. To conceive the true nature of every experience and to communicate its truth in words memorable and wholly expressive, is the poet's function. If it was a poet who imaged the mechanical process of nature in the figure of Jehovah, it was the priest who deified and systematised it, and imposed on men as an arbitrary sovereign what one of them had created as an image of natural experience.

Gods, then, we may well plead, have generally proved pitfalls to their worshippers. They have represented not a universal, but a particular phenomenon of life; they have stood for natural, or tribal, or even class experience. They may have been true enough symbols of particular energies, but they have been treated as comprehensive instead of partial and experimental symbols of life. They have most nearly represented human reason, and approximated least to brutal instinct, when the attributes of divinity have been reflected in a very enlightened human being. For a man, to impress his fellows, must at least demonstrate a wisdom greater than theirs. All bad religions, we may say, then, have been misapplied poetry, all good have centred around poetical men whose characters and utterances approximated most nearly to the ideals of poetry.

What, then, is the poet's ideal? Briefly this: to draw out of the material of life its ideal reality. In so doing, though his labour is always disinterested, he cannot, as a servant of life and beauty, fail to show where recalcitrant matter distorts the truth, and where it allows it free and harmonious expression. And thus, without consciously aiming at it, he should persuade men of the ideal necessity of ordering their lives in accordance with the rational harmony manifest in every creation of beauty and every act of self-forgetful virtue. When the poet represents vice, he does not falsify its nature by the exaggeration of panic and horror—indeed he will show, as even Milton does in the person of his Satan, the heroic attributes, the mental and physical vigour, which so often in the criminal suffer only from misdirection. If another Jehovah were created to-day, as a poetical image of nature and her ruthless methodical processes, the poet while portraying nature's physical grandeur would not attempt to persuade his audience to worship her as exclusively divine or emulate her primitive morality.

The aim of every religion, however, has been to discover and popularise some symbol which would both image the source of all organic life and offer to human beings a pattern of perfection. The two aspects have almost always in the past been confused to the prejudice alike of revelation and morality. And only of recent years has it been generally realised that the laws of nature and of man correspond, but do not coincide, that an economy of life applicable to a vegetable and an animal world is an outrage to a human and intelligent being, that if a God may be worshipped as the source and spirit of life, He can and must be controlled and directed by that human reason which is perhaps His highest expression. Man, in fact, is but now attaining his majority, and founding his own household; in that mansion he must recognise the responsibilities of godhead. He must at least be the human viceroy of a cosmic dispensation. The effect must transcend the cause.

All comparative religions have thus reflected the imperfections of man's evolution towards reason. They have been means to this end, and man's development has constantly outdistanced their uses, so that they have tended to retard his progress rather than accelerate it.

But poetry is an end in itself, for in all contemporary fact it should image the working of truth. The poet does not consciously wish to persuade anyone of the attractiveness of beauty, or the joyousness of virtue. His function is only to express these, to reveal them in being, as he reveals the terror of discord, or the ferocity of blind force. That true beauty must convert man to wisdom, humanity and joy, is for man to prove by submitting himself to the experience of art. The poet is occupied only in providing the true experience. He has no ulterior object. It is enough that the truth of life is a constant quality which the great poets of each generation should draw out of the different phenomena of their times. Heroic virtues generally find other ways of expressing themselves now than in the days of Homer— but their essential quality remains the same. Vice rarely displays such majestic enormity now as we witness in the days of the Borgias, but we detect a possible Count Cenci in every act of vicious, self-gratifying instinct.

Only, therefore, when men have accepted as a symbol of godhead some figure which represents not only the life principle ruthlessly repeating itself in nature, but also the perfected reason of man controlling nature's force, to produce a human harmony—only then will the poet admit religious faith to be identical with his own. For then mankind, if they translate their faith into action, will make of a material world a place of beauty, an ordered all-conscious human cosmos, like in its outlines and its rhythmic agreement to all great poetry, and to those ideal regions which every great poet has conceived and embodied, if perchance he might tempt man on to follow kindred laws and create a like perfection.

3

Yet it is the common supposition of men, emphatically logical, that the poet's idealism is not far removed from insanity, that at best it is a pleasant form of delusion well suited to entertain in an idle hour, but bearing little relation to the truth of practical life. We meet with this misconception on the lips of educated men no less than in the babble of vulgar opinion. Mr. Bingham, for example, writing in the *Westminster Review*, speaks of a man as being a " poet and therefore not a reasoner," and more recently a leader-writer in the *Times* sought to discredit the Poet Laureate's plea for reconciliation with German professors on the ground that, being a poet, he sacrificed his reason to his emotions. This opinion, we must admit, however false it be in the light of first principles, has only too often been justified in fact. Only the greatest poetry is found to be true both to life and to truth.

Particularly in the nineteenth century, with its unexampled fertility, do we find instances of poetry pursuing a superficial pleasure and cultivating a spurious charm. The passionate, if imperfect, idealism voiced by the Romantic writers early in the century, had quickly degenerated into sentiment, whether disguised as the sententiousness of the later Wordsworth, the delicate urbanity of Tennyson, the blunt optimism of Browning, or the self-absorbed preciosity of what became known as the *fin de siècle.* To use Aristotle's definition, the " frenzied man " had degenerated into the "accomplished man." With this we shall deal more in detail in a later chapter. It is enough to say here that every element of exaggeration and falsehood in poetry, whether emotional or intellectual, renders it perforce suspect in the eyes of thinking men, and also entails a reaction in which the neglected value is in its turn over-emphasised.

In the late Victorian Age the reaction was from sentiment to fact. We see men turning quite ruthlessly from the pleasant music of luxurious fancy to record life in its brutal actuality. For fear of false sentiment there was a revulsion even to physical ugliness. The century which began with a hasty idealism ends with a grovelling realism or a decorated dandyism.

But this fluctuation between unpondered aspiration and uninspired materialism, although it make poetry suspect, is no proof of the quixotry of idealism when truly realised. For if true idealism represents the highest consummation of human feeling and thought, a height from which it is easy to fall, and which because of the arduousness of its ascent often invites men to halt at some mid-point between fact and truth, pretending to an altitude which they have not attained, yet realism, a servile acceptance of the facts of life as material to be arranged by the calculating intelligence rather than to be related to an underlying unity, is, apart from the limitations which it imposes upon consciousness, no less dangerous a policy, in a world where primitive instincts still readily defeat logic and are therefore always destructive factors, unless creative idealism succeeds in spiritualising them.

For true idealism enlarges logic; it does not deny it. There is no contradiction in principle between imagination and reason. Utilitarian, metaphysical and creative thinkers differ only in the material upon which they work, that of the first being the facts marshalled by mechanical intelligence; of the second, factors abstracted from the phenomena of life, and systematised; of the third, life in all its particularities valued creatively and disinterestedly through the unification of the fact and the idea. The tendency of the utilitarian is to overlook the universal in the particular, of the philosopher to divorce his speculations from nature, sense, and humanity, of the idealist to neglect necessity in his impatience for sensational liberty. Therefore, while on the one side

D

we find Blake and Shelley imputing to reason all
the ugliness and evil of the world, and claiming for
imagination both a philosophic and a practical validity, on the other, among merchants, mechanicians,
political economists, and all self-termed practical men
of affairs, the exactly reverse opinion is current.
The poet's imagination is fancy to the practical
man, while the practical man's facts are irrelevant
to the poet.

True idealism should reconcile these two apparent
opposites. For the peculiar virtue of imagination
is that it combines the rational and the sensational
faculties, the mechanical mind and the natural
instinct. Thus the mind is rendered creative by
instinct, which embraces all life, denying distinctions, while uncritical instinct acquires form and
direction from association with the mind.

True imagination, therefore, is a combination of
passionate thought and physical sensation, and its
dispositions are absolutely true, because they represent the combined power of life and of thought,
the union of creation and perception. Such creative
perception is commonly named intuition, and because the reason inherent in it embraces and defines
a far wider landscape than logic alone can focus,
its rational consistency has been seldom recognised
by the narrowly logical. Moreover, the creative
element in intuition, through which the poet has
been enabled to sympathise with and penetrate

into all the active phenomena of life, compels him also to restore to concrete imagery the ideas which he has read in the matter of life. He does not, as the philosopher, convey his truth to others through the abstract formulas of a system of thought, but he creates a living organism, his poem, which embodies in its finer matter, with more decision and clearness than the grosser matter of nature will allow, the truth conceived by him from his intercourse with life. The poet's image then materialises his idea, and his idea is the significant reading of fact. But frequently to the mere logician neither image nor idea spell any conviction.

Further, as we shall show in the following studies, the exact agreement between the poet's sensation and his thought, in short the pure intuition, out of which the greatest art springs, is not a common occurrence. The finest poets have had to struggle for it, and often even in their work the balance is found to be inexact. The smaller poet may never attain to it for a single moment. For either the thought may be too weak to support the rush of powerful feeling, the blind naturalism of passion, as in such a poet as Swinburne, or the feeling may be wedded to perverse or prejudiced thought, and only serve to aggravate the error by the intensity with which it confirms it, as for example so often in Byron. Or again, the emotion may be so slight that it fails to liberate the reason, which remains narrowly critical instead of creative, as so often in the prose-poets of the eighteenth century, where the live image has degenerated into the conscious figure, or as in a decadent period when reason is solely occupied in arranging to the best effect the ornaments of a languid sensationalism. The poet has often proved false in all these directions, and merited the criticism of the philosopher, the utilitarian or the priest. Yet such failure does not prejudice the claims of true idealism, in which both the self is lost in the universe, and the universe re-composed by the self nearer to the heart's and the reason's estimate of values. Logic in itself is so short-sighted, so blind to wide issues and absolute values, that only by a more comprehensive process can we look for any consistent and comprehensive solution of those problems of both art and life which are in the last resort identical. Instinct alone reduces a man to the level of the species, thought alone divorces him from life. From the union of the two comes complete consciousness and so salvation.

4

In idealism, however, we may recognise two degrees, of which the first is best described in Goethe's own words. He says: " Our aesthetics speak a great deal of poetical or anti-poetical subjects;

fundamentally there is no subject that has not its poetry; it is for the poet to find it there."

From this aspect, idealism is as disinterested as science. It seeks only reality. The idealist conceives and expresses the essential nature of the phenomena before him. He experiences life with passionate sympathy, and, piercing through its forms, be they foul or fair in common opinion, he interprets their essence, just as the dramatist conceives and creates a host of characters different from and yet potential in his own. In this disinterested interpretation of life he is both realist and idealist. He does not criticise the particular expression of life before him; he accepts it, not, however, as fact, but in its ideal significance.

But from this imaginative neutrality a purer and more positive type of idealism is bound to evolve. We have said that the creative instinct inherent in imagination is as universal as it is uncritical, and leads a poet to merge the particular in the whole, to relate impressions isolated in space and time to an intuition which transcends both. This correlation of impressions, this linking of apprehension with comprehension, points inevitably to a realisation of what forces in life conduce to harmony or beauty, and what to discord and ugliness. The idealist becomes not only an unprejudiced recorder of the universal idea manifesting itself, however imperfectly or distortedly, in the particular, but an interpreter of the particular in its relation to the creative ideal, and himself a worshipper and, if possible, a creator of forms which reveal this creative ideal expressing itself in most positive harmony. He becomes in his desire for beauty a creative idealist, as in his essential record of ugliness he is a creative realist. Though he reveals discord and destruction where it exists in the experience of life, it is only to emphasise more powerfully the delight and wisdom of harmony, while both thought and memory are drawn upon by imagination to clothe and give body to this ideal intuition. Beauty is to him a passion more overwhelming than truth. For he has proved it to be the creative expression of truth. And only in the reconcilement of all discord within himself can he realise and so create pure beauty,—his highest function, as it is ultimately of the world.

For in ideal beauty, nature and reason, the infinite and the finite, unity and variety, liberty and law, form and matter, idea and image, thought and feeling, find agreement. Well might the poet cry of her rather than of gold, as did Timon in his bitterness:

> Thou visible God,
> That solder'st close impossibilities
> And mak'st them kiss! That speak'st with every tongue
> To every purpose! O, thou touch of hearts!

This, then, we conceive ultimately to be the religion of poetry. It is a religion of life, of men whose function it is neither to advise, to preach, nor to adjure, but only to create, first truly and then beautifully, and in each case passionately.

For the poet's ideas of truth spring from his emotional experience. And he restores them to a condition of emotion when he expresses them anew. Poetry offers, therefore, an escape from the material slavery, whether of licence or of logic. It should give us liberty of the highest degree, and, in its creation of intense forms of life in harmony, it provides man with an experience through which he can realise his faculties as a thinking and feeling being both vividly and morally. It teaches him the secret of pure delight, making him one with that creative spirit which religions have named God, while in its recognition of natural necessity, of the material limitations within which the creative spirit is compelled to express itself, it teaches him how to reconcile his infinite aspiration, his improvident desire, with finite conditions and rational requirements. The poet, we would reiterate, has himself no aim other than a pure expression of truth, an absolute realisation of experience, and, as a higher consequence of this, a perfect creation of beauty.

But this ultimate function of his as a beauty-maker, as one who transcends the conditions of nature and creates a form of life purer than is to be found in the world, needs emphasising. For in these days the poet's duty as a critical realist is often announced, to the exclusion of his duty as a creative idealist; his business as a revealer of things as they are is more often quoted than his distinction as a creator of things as they ought to be. The true poet is philosopher, psychologist and moralist, but all to an absolute degree; above all he is a man spurred on by high passions, championing the deepest and truest values in the face of society and circumstance, and all the grinding logic of the world. His example should serve both to call men back to nature and speed them on to truth. He is no literary manikin tasting the pleasures of cultivated emotions or paddling in the stream of private sensations. He is one with the creative spirit of life, and the world that is and that is to be mingle in his utterance. He is at his highest " the prophetic soul of the world dreaming on things to come "; for the end of the world too is surely beauty.

Poetry, then, is an intenser and more purified revelation of nature by the genius of man. Yet though the idealist's aim be no more than absolute expression, and though at first many find the poet's creation no more enlightening than they find nature's own landscape, those who will discipline themselves to the experience will discover great poetry to be what few religions have ever been—true both to life and to thought, delightful, and in an absolute sense moral in so far as it images truth and refines a temperament by advertising both the energy of life and the wisdom of its right directions. Above all, true poetry is a discloser of the eternal in time.

All great art is indirectly both didactic and religious, for it teaches men by its influence and example how to live truly and how to die with hope. We are bettered by our intercourse with it, as we are by an intimacy with a man of high intelligence and refined sensibility. We are brought by it into a condition of true liberty, our emotions are purged, our passions chastened, our reason advances beyond logic to essential perception, our whole being is translated into a world rich, measured, calm and majestic, a world in which neither meanness nor incontinence, feebleness nor shame, discord nor languor, perversity nor narrow-mindedness exist.

The heaven of great art is then the offspring of creative idealism, and if because of his passionate nature the artist, when his passion lacks governance, may prove the subtlest and most compelling aid to depravity and excess, in his truth he is the most completely, the most alluringly true of all men. His ethics are absolute, for they are one with the pure air of heaven, the mounting sun, the budding hedgerows, the noblest achievements of man.

CHAPTER II

THE EMERGENCE OF MORALITY

Wherever he stands, at the beginning or the end of things, a man has to sacrifice his gods to his passions, or his passions to his gods. That is the problem, great enough, in all truth, if approached in the spirit of sincerity and knowledge.—JOSEPH CONRAD.

I

WE have said that absolute poetry represents a marriage of the senses and the mind, a marriage so perfect in its harmony that the fact of its dualism serves only to produce a high and comprehensive unity, in which the cold formality of reason, and the impulsive energy, the sympathetic tenderness of emotion unite. " Nature has kissed art," as Mr. Bridges has worded it, and the child of these nuptials is poetry.

Poetry cannot do without either of its parents, and in its attempts to deny one of them has often enough courted either the death of physical nature or the lifelessness of mental conceit. So far as we can see, we cannot even be exclusively spiritual on this earth without courting sickness and at last death. If spirituality entails a progressive starving of the body, a surrender of the will to abstract

32

ideals, a resting upon consoling sentiments—it quickly becomes a pestilence-stricken miasma, clouding the brain, thinning the blood, withering the senses. Lust itself, we are driven to admit, is preferable to spiritual anaemia, since it contains at least the potentialities of life. The senses are the instrument upon which the spirit must play. The instrument may be more and more finely strung, but it must never be broken or thrown aside. An analogy therefore must always exist between the activity of nature and of the poet. Human intelligence cannot define the creative force manifest in nature's ever-variant imagery: philosophers have indeed denied to such phenomena material existence; they have made all things not only the measure, but the substance of human mind. But the poet who, like Dr. Johnson kicking a stone to refute Berkeley, is convinced of the existence of a natural world external to himself, discovers nature's methods to be kindred to his own. She, in her affluence, in her joyous energy, in her destructiveness, in her triumph of form over reckless confusion, would seem to reveal both a creative and critical intelligence at work in physical matter. In the soft colour of deepening twilight, in the brilliance of a frosty morning, in the involved tracery of a soaring tree, in the agreed company of the stars, we seem to detect the expression alike of a cosmic energy and a great master mind. Yet nature's material is physical, and her criterion of value is force. Her harmony is the balance of forces, her discord their battle. The life-energy contains in itself an equal tendency towards order and towards chaos, and order triumphs only by the extermination of the superfluous. Nature is both divine and satanic: divine at the expense of numberless organisms which she is compelled to destroy, because her creative desire outruns her formative discretion. Her life only persists within the vicious circle of thriftless creation and destruction. She lives in a perpetual whirl and without it she would perish terribly. She is like a vast crowd in a narrow lane, that must keep moving; in her, love and hate are indistinguishable, for they are both the exultant expression of a self-absorbed life-force.

Yet man himself is the proof that within her creative principle the germ of reason lurks. Man is nature made conscious of intelligence, and it is thus that he has risen slowly above the natural economy into which he was born. His distinctive humanity is comprised in this alone, that while still loyal to nature's creative principle, her joy and passion for life, he, by the harmonious exercise of his faculties, under the direction, at first conscious and then habitual, of reason, may enthrone the mind's values over the body's, the spiritual over the physical, the idea over the fact. In short he realises nature on a higher plane. Thus, to take a particular example, the poet in his creative activity is as profligate in his conceptions as nature herself, with the difference that his matter is ideal instead of physical. Thoughts, emotions, and their counterpart words and images, throng his consciousness, crying for expression, and he is compelled to reject a hundred in the interests of one. He displays all nature's uncritical sensibility, moving headlong from image to image, combining elements and resolving them in a perpetual flux, ultimately to form by selection something outside the friction of movement and above the fickleness of change, something organic of which each element is in harmony with its fellow.

And in a more general sense mankind has increasingly admitted it to be the supreme aim of humanity for the individual to govern his actions by the light of more than private discretion, to reconcile his desires, which in origin are promiscuous and universal, with those of others, rather than to obtain a personal triumph by the use of force, a personal survival by the slaughter of his neighbour.

In the development then and realisation of reason as a faculty commensurate with sensation, the history of both art and civilisation is contained, and the two are intimately connected. The evolution alike of mankind and of individual poets bears witness to it. The slow emergence of true human values in the life of society offers a close analogy to the development of poetry, which is the highest expression of humanity. We shall see how in art, reason is to begin with subservient to instinct, serving only as an instrument to induce order among crowded sensation; and how later, having become positive, it directs and utilises sensation to arrive at ideal truth beyond the transient and material. Man, in short, advances from a surrender to natural beauty to an apprehension of intellectual beauty. He uses his animal instincts to transcend space and time, and enlarges his humanity until it touches the divine.

2

The growth of idealism is perhaps most visibly revealed, first in the advance of man from primitive conditions to some form of social life, and secondly in the triumph of Christianity over Paganism. We need hardly say that neither social nor Christian principles are in any sense practised to-day. Everywhere we see man surrendering to primitive instinct, and attempting to defend by mere casuistry purely pagan actions. But social and Christian conceptions prove that man's consciousness is alive to idealism, however much the ideas are disregarded or abused in practice.

The primitive man was, however, the mental because the physical slave of necessity; to him instinct was paramount, and in his simple animal existence, force, as in nature, was the only logic. Yet anthropologists tell us that the dimensions of the savage's brain were little different from those

of the man of to-day, and that the whole of progress
lies in the growth of man's consciousness of his
brain's existence, and so of his exercise of it. Certainly the significant form revealed often in the
mere scrawls of the primitive artist go far to support
the theory, that as in nature and the child, so in the
savage a potential reason exists, which can inform
the irregular creations of instinct with the pure
reality of rational design. In this the art of the
savage was not unlike his life, in which a natural
heroism manifests itself among conditions generally
brutal. It was because, like nature, the savage lived
thoughtlessly in the moment that he was both
criminal and heroic. Pain and death meant as little
to him as to his ox, because he was blind to their
moral significance. Nor did the exploitation of his
passions at first involve a vast catastrophe. For if
a social order existed, it was of a very slender and
fluid nature, while even man's instruments of
destruction were so ineffectual that they added little
to his limited capacity to do his neighbours injury.
But a more fixed society, evolving both out of man's
creative and possessive instinct, which urged him
first to unite with his fellows, and then to protect
the union once formed, encouraged him to supplement power by ingenuity. If only to further licence
or self-satisfaction, cunning grew out of force, the
germ of reason in the matter of instinct. But when
cunning became with strength a quality common to

many, rather than the privilege of the shrewder few, it was forced upon the dawning reason of the savage that the unregulated exercise of both tended to conflict with the interests of all alike, and as soon as he discovered the unfettered pursuit of his desires to endanger even more than it gratified his own person, he began to exercise his cunning in defending himself against others, and in so doing created the machinery by which others might defend themselves against him. Out of this self-interested compact sprang the primitive social state. The wild instincts which, in a small wandering tribal people, could express themselves immediately, because both the range of destructiveness and the occasion for revenge were limited, were recognised in a settled community to be dangerous both to the individual who exploited them and to the society which suffered them, even as the forces of wind and water, which can do so little injury to the forest, can destroy the wattled hut. The heroic gestures which men could safely make when only the horizon hemmed them in, proved little suited to the dimensions of four walls. And so because the general and the particular interests coincided, the morality of the primitive state took shape, a rule of law within which the powerful could still express themselves, but with comparative immunity from dangerous consequences, and with an ever-heightening sense of what power should aim at achieving. On this basis a pagan civilisation was reared, and has persisted until our own day. For Christian ideals have scarcely yet begun to affect the political or economic relations of communities to any notable degree. The pagan state quite candidly admitted the validity of force, but took measures to guard the interested individual or community against its unprofitable excesses. By a balance and arrangement of forces men induced a certain order out of chaos, without in any way transcending the logic of force. They had reached, in short, that point of rational consciousness which could direct instinct to the attainment of its own advantage. But they did not question the right of instinct to be the only judge of what true advantage was. This imperfect social morality then, evolved as a protection against the immediate depredations of primitive instinct, was scarcely worthy of the name of morality at all, in so far as reason in it was still only an instrument subservient to the ends of instinct, and likely indeed to delay the adoption of a true morality because it protected men against the worst consequences of a false. In true morality man recognises that many of nature's values are not humanity's, and that human happiness is only to be won by the rational control and direction of nature's forces towards ideal ends. In the pagan state the fact had certainly been brought home even to the powerful:

> Alas! when evil men are strong
> No life is good, no pleasure long.

E

But they had realised it as a fact, not as a truth, and their morality consisted only in modifying the fact where it imperilled themselves, not in denying or transcending it. And so centuries of brutality had to pass before even the most enlightened among them became like the Clifford of the same poem:

> He, long forced in humble walks to go,
> Was softened into feeling, soothed and tamed.
> Love had he found in huts where poor men lie;
> His daily teachers had been woods and rills,
> The silence that is in the starry sky,
> The sleep that is among the lonely hills.
> In him the savage virtue of the Race,
> Revenge and all ferocious thoughts were dead;
> Nor did he change; but kept in lofty place
> The wisdom which adversity had bred.

Yet if the morality dictated by the more obvious needs of social life was insignificant and untrustworthy, certain limits were at least imposed upon the sovereignty of nature, and man's first attempt to restrain an instinct because he realised the injury which it would entail, if only to himself, or that enlargement of himself—the community to which he belonged,—represented his first assertion of ideal values. Even this humble consciousness of self-interest was bound, however, to be capricious, while man's understanding of both nature and himself was yet so limited that he was rarely competent to judge where it was prudent to follow nature and where to rebel, and while forethought was still so unpractised that it was easily overwhelmed by any powerful impulse. Human reason has in fact developed so slowly that even to-day we constantly see in intelligent men's utterance the unpondered acquisitiveness of the animal scantily veiled in a tissue of logic or of prejudiced sentiment.

Doubtless, however, primitive man is so little removed from a state of nature that his very survival depends on a more cunning exploitation of her principles. To transcend them at such an early stage would inevitably entail his material destruction.

The first aim, therefore, of morality was to preserve the individual from avoidable physical injury and to further his selfish interests. But as a result of this a tradition of social habit conducive to orderly life was formed, and was later embodied and elaborated in a code of law, until with the establishment of a comparative security it was possible for the choicest spirits to contemplate a higher form of life; first, to apprehend the reality of nature, her ferocity and her beauty, and secondly, to mount to rational reality, to conceive an ideal humanity, and to interpret life anew from that standpoint.

Man's physical and moral development are then closely allied, the one indeed at first dictating the other. The savage in his struggle for survival is solely occupied in devising means of protection against the forces of nature, the ravages of wind and water, the onslaughts of the beasts that prowl by night. Only after much experience can he learn the habitual nature of these forces and the best way to circumvent them. And not until he has constructed solid defences against them has he the power or the taste to adorn these defences or experiment in more graceful structures. It is so with man's morality. He is engaged first in discovering those instincts which, if unrestrained, will harm primarily himself and secondarily others. He is next occupied in controlling them by an exercise of forethought; he develops his reason in the process. Only then is he at liberty to turn his mind to the abstract study of nature's reality, and later to the positive task of conceiving and realising conditions of life which answer to his ideal. We shall see how in the evolution of art this development from a condition in which the artist is occupied almost wholly in ordering and expressing nature to one in which he interprets ideas more essential than nature, holds good. For one of the main purposes of our argument is to prove that idealism is to be traced equally in the growth of an art of life, as of an art of art. But in the province of active life we must admit that, with the exception of certain enlightened civilisations, for brief periods and within very limited areas, man cannot be said to have yet realised either an efficient natural morality, or to have begun to base his policy or his social ethics on ideal principles. Peoples who tolerate or encourage the exploitation of human energy in a soulless competitive system are little further removed from the processes of nature than those who exist by perpetual warfare. The predatory instinct, we may say, has been legalised; it has never been candidly denied a place in the economy of life. Rather it has been translated into terms of enterprise, business and initiative, and as such has been applauded. By some modern philosophy it has been actually exalted into a creed. Yet generally in man's philosophy and sentiment, as distinct from his practice, an advance from brutal assertiveness and sensual satisfaction towards rational ideality has always been visible, and if Christianity has done little to restrain the policies of nations, in whom pagan instincts have often merely been intellectualised, it has profoundly affected individuals, and its phenomenal acceptance as the religious creed of the modern world proves that it answers more completely than paganism to the often latent but progressive consciousness of humanity.

The manifestation of Christ's humanism, as distinct from pagan distortions of His doctrine, has been only less gradual in the progressive idealism of art than in the practice of life, yet that pregnant sentence, " God is Love," interpreted though it might often seem to have been as " God is Lust," contains without doubt the truth which divides the art and life of the pagan world, of Greece and the Renaissance, from that of a world no less ardent but more mature, a world which was born with the Reformation and reached its adolescence with the Revolution.

3

It would of course be absurd to attempt to date in any narrow sense the existence of pagan and Christian conceptions of life. For firstly, only a minute fraction of any generation entertains a definite conception of life at all: and secondly, amongst that small band of highly conscious men, poets, thinkers and men of leisure, many are original enough to differ from conventional creeds, outstripping time in their realisation of thought, as an athlete outruns competitors less highly specialised.

It is evident enough, for example, that the words in which Socrates describes the supreme Beauty in the *Phædrus* and the *Symposium* are ideally in advance of the conception of Beauty entertained by Chaucer or the early Puritans, or the vast majority of Christian theologians; that Greek and other myths are full of a symbolical reading of the cosmos and of organic nature, to which modern philosophy and science have but recently attained by a more laborious route; that such an ancient custom, for example, as the torch-race, with which Plato's *Republic* opens, had as highly moral a significance as any of Christ's own parables, advertising as it did that the race is not to the swift, but to the wise. On the other side,

not only actions which have pleaded Christianity
as their excuse, but dogmas and practices which
men, calling themselves Christians, have reconciled
with their creed, could be quoted without number
to show that Christianity has often proved more
brutally pagan than paganism itself. Such contradictions are unavoidable: for in the slow and
quixotic evolution of mankind, a few are always to
be found far in advance of their age's consciousness,
while the many are invariably far behind. Yet
viewed comprehensively, we believe that an increasingly conscious distinction between the pagan
idea of life and the Christian can be traced beneath
the apparent paganism of modern European civilisation, and that in this alone can the modern world be
said to surpass the ancient. If, however, the ethics
which have governed the policies of nations, and
the economies of societies, should still seem primarily
pagan, the spirit of modern literature, the profound
humanity which has increasingly transcended the
limits of a narrow, if graceful, humanism, attests
beyond doubt a very marked enlargement of spiritual
consciousness. Essentially paganism differs from
Christianity in this. The pagan desires to realise
himself through conflict, to absorb physically and
dominate every form of life which he meets.
Primarily he is hungry and would appease his
appetite; secondarily, through the resistance offered
by the matter which he would subdue, he enjoys

a sense of his own power, and thereby a certain degree of consciousness. Love therefore for him is in its simplest kind lust, and at its highest is all entangled in hate. The γλυκυπικρος Ἔρως of the Greek or that querulous cry of Catullus:

Odi et amo: quare id faciam, fortasse requiris.
Nescio, sed fieri sentio et excrucior.

reflect this entanglement, from which the limited Pagan consciousness, however refined its intellect, could not escape.

The Christian, by contrast, wishes to attain consciousness by giving himself to all things, realising life through sympathy and understanding rather than domination. In so doing ideally he does not sacrifice his identity, but only enlarges and heightens it by a continuous reinforcement from the diverse elements of life about him. He refuses to destroy or suppress life, in the manner of the pagan, because he recognises in all things a potential part of himself, which he is loath to eliminate spiritually by subjecting physically.

The distinctive feature therefore of modern art is that its impulse is one of cultivation rather than exploitation. It tends to spring from men who have sublimated possessive greed into disinterested creativeness, who no longer wish to enforce their will upon life, but through understanding to evoke beauty from life, and whose sense of beauty is no longer submerged in the material, but discriminatingly spiritual.

It must be remembered, too, that we see the pagan world complete as a cycle reflecting certain energies, passing through certain phases, and in good time, having realised all its potentialities, coming to an inevitable end. The Christian world, on the other hand, is still in its infancy, though men viewing the decay of conventional religion may falsely deem its ideal disproved. The truth is that the idea of Christianity which in its purity is also the inspiration of art, was first consciously apprehended by poets, with certain singular exceptions to whom we shall refer, only a century and a half ago, while it is at this very moment only beginning to affect the practical affairs of life, to influence the relationships of men and nations, because necessity, as she has ever done, is forcing man's intelligence to admit that a higher conception of life will serve best his material interest, his desire for survival and for physical well-being.

For almost all man's evolution from lower to higher planes of consciousness may be traced to the physical suffering consequent on a failure to govern his actions by the light of pure and rational humanity; and his spiritual evolution should therefore become more rapid as his powers increase, the excesses of instinct proving the more ruinous as he advances from a simple physical to a materially complex form of life.

Laying aside then the terms Pagan and Christian, which we have used thus far because they denote respectively a natural and a spiritual conception of life, we may say that the ancient world was one in which sensation predominated, in which men accepted the limitations of instinct, ennobling and refining it, while in the modern world for seven hundred years the mind of man has been discovering itself as a decisive faculty, and has led him to pursue, often mistakenly, an ideal of liberty by which he might escape the comfortless flux of the phenomenal world; this reason has been constantly engulfed in the tide of organic life, has united in rare moments with sensation to achieve a pure intuition, and at last in these latter days is becoming conscious of its duty, its power and its destiny.[1]

The ideal of the ancient world was natural, that of the modern is moral. We have not forgotten the Delphic precept, " Know thyself " — but that was at best an imperfect maxim and one upon which the ancient world in general acted even less manifestly than the modern. To the pagan, nature was enough because she was everything; he was of her household as a child, that scarce questioned his own identity. With a courage heroic in its blind surrender to the momentary, he accepted life and death without considering their implications. Life maybe was brief and the creature perishable, but he was born into a

[1] I read in a leader of *The Times* to-day this sentence: " We are but at the very beginning of the knowledge and control of our minds; but with that beginning an immense hope is dawning upon the world."

glorious dawn, and he was content merely to accept the excitement of experience. An uncrowded world still allowed of an existence in which the physical creature could exult and the animal faculties expand, in which the mind had not yet been forced by pain even to the point of self-consciousness, and man was still far removed from the subtleties of self-question-ing or the morbidities of self-disgust. Where reason functioned it served to give to an ardent sensuality ever more precise expression, ever richer harmony, interposing with temperate persuasion between life and licence. To the pagan the infinite was only a multiplication or aggrandisement of the finite, the ideal a heightened actuality. Their gods had all the animal virtues and vices; they were subject to the creature's frailties and exploited the creature's passions. They did not generally suffer for their vices, because the pagan genius which created them was too gladly instinctive and indeed found it easy to forget that death and anguish are the wages of sin. For nature suffers without knowing it, and the Greek gods are the forces and beauties of nature personified.

Even in the Greek drama, where we find the pagan mind most conscious of the unknown, the dark destiny which seems to lie in wait for the children of men and exploit their strength and frailty, tyrannises little less over the gods themselves, who are the slaves of a weak malignity and an insatiate appetite, and who if they rebel against the rigid celestial constitution of the time, are doomed to a punishment no less grim than is the lot of mortals. The highest intelligence of antiquity admitted the possibility of rebellion, and embodied the protest of reason against authority, of life against convention, in the noblest of tragedies. But Aeschylus, like the author of Genesis, considers it ideally just though pitiable that the rebel should be branded both criminal and outcast. Both Prometheus and our first parents in Eden have ever been considered to have denied God, in asserting the right of human reason and their own individuality, whereas in truth they should be regarded as the first champions of divine humanity in the face of brutal nature.

Of the modern conception of love too the pagan was incapable. Life was his only love, rather than, as with the mystic of a later day, love his only life. The goddess of Love, Aphrodite, daughter of the Syrian Astarte, held sway over a humble kingdom, and her morals often accorded with it. It is a later sentiment which has attached to her the synonym of Beauty. To the ancients she was rather the pure emblem of desire, the servant of the creative instinct. Indeed the self-gratifying values of paganism are nowhere so clearly indicated as in the Greek attitude to women. Even so sophisticated a writer as Euripides can conceive of no relation between men and women save the exclusively sexual, upon which therefore his cynical wit is driven to play. Not

until the late Greek romancers of the second century
(particularly Longus) do we find any delicate sentiment associated with the weaker sex. And not
until Virgil, and even in him fitfully, do we meet
with that first blend of mysticism, sentiment and
naturalism which was to grow in the Middle Ages
into a fine, if sometimes decadent, flower of devotion, and develop from an artistic convention
into a habitual attitude in the highest modern
conception of human passion.

In brief, then, the pagan, accepting nature from
within, found satisfaction in an animal well-being,
of which his art gives an ideal representation. But
although each moment seems imperishable to those
who taste life through the senses, none are more
subject to the law of physical growth and decay.
Pagan art and life are complete, and within their
limits perfect, where modern art and life are incomplete and imperfect; but because they expressed
a lower aim and embodied only a natural consciousness, they budded, flowered and died like a physical
organism, and it was left for later ages to develop
the germ of reason latent in antiquity, pursuing,
however darkly and capriciously, a higher and more
personal destiny.

With the passing of Greek and Roman civilisation,
darkness for a time closed in upon the world. Indeed,
looking back upon them from our standpoint, the
ages of classical life and learning appear as an

enclosed garden, in which for a short period humanity realised an inspired childhood before the full and bitter battle of life was made known to it. After the convulsion of migrating peoples had shattered the defences of city states and the ensuing chaos had begun to take form in feudalism and nationalism, finer spirits could no longer luxuriate in the bright sunlight of a sequestered paradise. Life had revealed to them the ravages of its lust: their sense had learnt to suffer more often than to enjoy, and in the stress of pain reason grew apace. And as if to guide and encourage the dawning consciousness of free-will, the deprecating voice of Christianity sounded its mournful challenge, proclaiming suffering as the inevitable but glorious incident of this earthly pilgrimage, but heralding a glad eternity beyond the grave. We hear this new and wistful note even in so earthly tolerant a poet as Chaucer:

> Flee from the press, and dwell with soothfastness . . .
> That thee is sent, receive in buxomness,
> The wrestling for this world asketh a fall,
> Here is no home, here is but wilderness:
> Forth, Pilgrim, forth! Forth, beast, out of thy stall!
> Know thy countree, look up, thank God of all;

or again:

> O youngë freshë folkës, he or she,
> In which that love upgroweth with your age,
> Repair ye home from worldly vanitie,
> And of your heart upcast ye the visage
> To that same God that after His image
> You made; and think that all is but a fair,
> This world, that passeth soon as flowers fair.

Christianity thus divides in the history of man's
mind the period of joyous physical satisfaction from
that of sadness and subliminal aspiration. Its teaching directed men's minds away from the life of the
senses and offered them ideal consolation for those
material pains and disappointments which now
wounded a more delicate sensibility. To men conscious of life's tragedy the world became a place of
error and fear, and they transferred their hopes to
the remote sanctuary of either an imaginative or a
fanciful heaven. Thus, while the ancient world is
devoted to nature and limited by her, yet within
these limits perfectly idealises her, the mediæval
world withdrew a pace from her in a first baffled
disillusionment, and devoted its energies above all
to decoration, to the adornment of life by human
fancy in place of the antique representation of her
by inspired instinct. The mediævalist imposed a
personal and fanciful art upon nature: he did not
attempt to make his sentiment for beauty coincide
with the realities of life. We see, for example, in
all the parade and pageantry of chivalry an ideal
of purity and grace superficially conceived and
often dwindling into a meaningless affectation and
but thinly veiling a brutal licence. It is the same
with the decoration lavished upon mediæval art,
of which indeed so much poetry of the period was
entirely composed. Whether it be the fair convention of the " Rose " applied to womanhood or the

grotesque gargoyle in its Gothic niche — these are
conceits bearing little relation to life except in so
far as they contradict or caricature it, and their
appeal lies almost entirely in the manner—gracious
or grotesque as that may be.   The same absence
of inquisitive egotism, the same satisfaction with
the superficial æsthetic values of decoration is
apparent in many of the Renaissance painters.   In
Raphael's " Crucifixion," for example, the technique
of colour and form is exquisite, but of the tragedy
or triumph of the crucified Christ nothing is conveyed.   Indeed by this criterion the whole picture
is an irrelevance.   The agreeably poised angels, the
attitudinised mourners, even the smiling landscape,
are a denial of the agony and infamy of the scene.
The artist is in fact indulging his sense of beauty
at the expense of truth; he is using an eternal tragedy
as a means to perfect brushwork, as a frame to his
own delight in the physical world and a mood of
elegant devotion.   With so purely æsthetic an activity
we may contrast the vivid, enquiring personality,
the critical truth, evident in such a modern portrait
as Epstein's " Christ."   It was, however, by the
indulgence of fancy that humanity became distinctively aware of itself.   And although, when man
advanced from the confusion of the Dark Ages to
the comparative stability of sovereign states, we still
find a physical conception of life predominant, we
find also the germ of self-conscious reason active

as it never was before in the religious faith of men,
and liable more and more to find full expression
in poetry. Men had learnt to rebel against naturalism
or realism, whether embodied in feudalism or
religious dogma. They had become conscious of
their human rights, because the years had so long
and so savagely denied them, and Protestantism
only set the seal of authority upon a condition which
history had determined. The finite world, which
had satisfied the ancients because it was good to
live in, ceased to be enough for men when it starved
them or put them to torture. They demanded
another in which such things might not be, and
imagination supplied it. In the mind of highly
sensitive and injured men there sprang up an image
of perfection cherished safe beyond the cruel indiscretion of mortal events; for every ugly thing
these souls created a beautiful, and for an earth
in which pain played the tyrant they built a heaven
where " sorrow and sighing shall pass away." For
centuries it did not trouble men that this perfect
province of the imagination should correspond but
little with the actual world. They cherished it as
a private place of refuge, the more safe because
actuality scarcely touched it at a single point. It
was a dream rather than a vision.

The religious-minded, however, speedily degraded
their dream in their attempt to convert the world;
they became hard and dogmatic, and more cruel

F

in the desire to reform than the nature that was their adversary. But poets were generally wiser: at worst they remembered the ideal from time to time, and escaped either the licence or the dogma that would degrade them in the pure harmony of their art as art, and more rarely in the realisation of an eternal conception. All the great poets of our literature from Chaucer's time, and many a lesser poet in his highest moments, attained, amidst much that was a surrender to brutal instinct or a denial of pure imagination, a true apprehension of nature, and an artistic mastery of their matter. Only a few rose to the height of an ideal, as distinct from a fanciful, conception of what human life might be in its perfection.

But in the late eighteenth century we find poets beginning definitely to relate their ideal to actuality, at first in a simple and domestic manner, but in ever widening circles, until the absolute values of an imaginative heaven and the degraded values of a social and political world are brought into close conflict, and the bravest minds of the early nineteenth century, basing their ardent hopes of regeneration on a belief in the infinite perfectibility of the human race, foretell a time when the ideal and the fact may indeed be one.

4

The distinction, then, between a Christian and a pagan conception of life, although too dimly defined in human consciousness to affect strongly man's practical policies, has increasingly manifested itself as a leaven working in the lump both of life and of art. And since art at its crudest is removed one step at least away from the material and towards the ideal, we can trace most clearly the difference between ancient and modern consciousness by a general reference to the distinctive symptoms revealed in the art and particularly the poetry of each. Ancient art we find then in the first place accepting the finite, even when it reflects the cosmic, modern seeking the infinite. The one moves on an equable plane of joyous content or patient submission, avoiding extremes and expressing the natural harmony of a healthy, limited organism; the other suffers physically for its spiritual intensity; it knows the malady of transcendentalism, and because the reason is not yet master of experience nor the physical world yet reconciled with its spiritual ideal, we find in it the aggravated extremes of ecstasy and dis-illusionment, we discover men to have become sufficiently individual to have lost touch with a natural harmony without as yet attaining a spiritual. Modern art, then, is less perfect than ancient because it aims higher and has a vaster discord to resolve, that, namely, of the human values and those of the organic universe. Ancient art on the whole attempted to resolve nature's discords, as nature resolved them herself. It therefore tends towards the impersonal, because the mind of the artist accepts the matter of nature, criticising it only in the formal exercise of his craft, while modern art has grown more and more individualistic as human reason has disputed the sovereignty of the actual. Ancient art represents a refined sensuality, modern an effort of individual imagination, an attempt to capture a higher synthesis, in which intelligence and instinct combine. The passive morality too of the ancient world was a sublimation of animal stoicism, while its highest ethic, the emphasis which it laid upon discipline and restraint, defined by Greek philosophers in the word σωφροσύνη, or by the Romans in "virtus," was directly traceable to its instinctive worship of physical health and efficiency, which it translated into terms of conduct, and named morality. Modern morality, however, at its best demands spiritual health as of infinite worth in itself, and even admits that it may exist independently of physical efficiency. Beyond a stoical endurance of natural evil, it claims a mastery of circumstance by the human spirit triumphing in its own self-sufficient power, and beyond a merely prudent restraint of natural excess, it claims an absolute expression through nature of rational values. It is positive where ancient morality was negative, spiritual instead of sensational, discriminating rather than dogmatic. Perhaps nowhere is the contrast between the two more evident than in their conception of Nature. The Greek mythology is an example of marvellous idealisation of natural forces, whether of air, earth, water, or fire. Its creators were what many primitive artists are, inspired scientists, and the exact and intricate symbolism through which they expressed the facts of the organic universe is astoundingly confirmed by modern science. But they attempted no universal synthesis; their reason was content to accept such a loose and heterogeneous system of warring energies as Nature at first sight suggests. They did not compel her into the unity of their own minds, and her forces remained a cluster of fortuitous particulars. The modern mind has, however, effected this synthesis: it has substituted theism or pantheism for polytheism, and in the whole economy of Nature it sees a spirit striving for fuller and more perfect expression, of which the process is evolution, and of which man is perhaps the crowning achievement.

The pagan then, being as it were a pulse of Nature, reflected her uncritically and reproduced and magnified her fact. He did not, as the modern, view her rationally, and either criticise her vices by the light of his own mind, or accuse his own meanness by the light of her ideal principles. He neither loved nor hated, but accepted her. We see this particularly in the Greek's love and practice of the plastic arts, since the imitation of the human form in stone is nearer to the conditions of actual life than its portrayal on canvas, where perspective interposes a human artifice between the fact and its representation. And if we contrast their conception of man in stone with, to take an extreme example, that of Mestrovich, we realise how perfect an agreement existed in the Greek mind between sense and spirit, between life as the flesh embodied it and as the mind desired it. For the ideality of Greek art consisted in a discreet imitation of the fact. Every quality of physical beauty discoverable in the human form was concentrated in an ideal representation, one in which no disproportion was allowed to exist. Sometimes in the image the sense of strength or of grace predominates, just as these artists created the same god from different aspects, but the configuration was borrowed directly from life, if reared on a more majestic scale and combining all physical perfection. The natural to them was indeed the reasonable, matter and mind were not yet divorced, the artist had no need either to reveal or transcend mutilations of the physical which time and circumstance had not yet wrought. But how rarely the modern finds Nature and humanity, virility and grace thus at peace with one another! There is apparent a divorce, sometimes terrible, between the physical and the spiritual. Reason in its growth, imperfect though progressive, has destroyed the balance of Nature, and the modern artist is torn between three visions, one of Nature in her antique and physical simplicity; one of man as he so generally is now, the battle-ground of warring forces, of Nature that demands harmony even by brutality, and of understanding that narrowly and morally discriminates; and one of the ideal reconciliation of the future, when reason, full-grown and conscious, shall unite once again with a reinstated Nature in a synthesis such as the old world with all its natural sensibility, inspired animalism, and youthful energy could not conceive, since the human still served the physical. In that ultimate consciousness of which many of our poets and such a novelist as Dostoievsky have given expression, the grace of art, the truth of wisdom, the strength and simplicity of Nature shall merge together. Pleasure shall no longer be the adversary of purity, nor wit of wisdom, nor thought of life, but the genius of an enlightened humanity, as responsive to sensation as it is heedful of discretion, shall ensure that the art of art and of life shall be one.

5

The art of the ancients, however, was subject to the common limitations of all natural organisms. It was like a flower, which by intensive culture might be refined, but in the process of refinement was bound to lose its vigour and eventually decay. Such is the fate of all sensationalism. Modern art, which is a hybrid representing the conscious dualism of Nature and humanity, is assured of a far greater permanence, since either of its two elements, if exaggerated, stimulates the growth of its opposite, and so the balance of health is maintained, reason checking the excesses of instinct, and instinct modifying the negativeness of reason. Thus in the development, for example, of our own literature, we see periods of growth, maturity and decadence, of action and reaction: but all such cycles are subservient, when viewed from a wider standpoint, to a measured and regular advance towards the realisation of a more complete consciousness and a more absolute and comprehensive ideal. The best instance, perhaps, of the limitations of pagan art is to be found in the Greek drama. It is the child of Homer, and Homer is universal Nature. His gods are personified forces, his heroes are noble, at times even subtle, animals. Æschylus borrowed from Homer particular myths and legends which he elaborated, condensed, and a little humanised. He reared his drama upon the animal passions of men, embodied both in themselves and in gods who either compelled man from without to indulge ruinous passions, or were themselves the cruel agents of retribution. The morality lay in a recognition of the natural law by which force germinates force, and acts contrary to reason, surrenders to momentary instinct, enslave a human being to the processes everywhere visible in the natural world. That such temptations to passion could be reasonably resisted was never suggested of characters whose physical heroism rendered the catastrophe the more sentimentally sublime. We say " sentimentally sublime " with purpose. For true sublimity does not lie in the defeat of physical strength by physical disaster, but in the triumph of a man's moral grandeur over the worst that a material world can inflict on his body—the triumph of a Milton, for example, over his blindness and indigence. But in Greek drama, although of course there are examples of such moral grandeur, Fate, not character, was the supreme deity of the imagination, representing, in fact, little more than physical instincts which man had not learnt to control, while the pagan conception of virtue lay generally in an heroic submission to, or an unflinching exaction of, the penalties consequent on misguided actions. To say this is not to forget that the very servile sense of necessity which created alike the Eumenides, incestuous Œdipus, Clytemnestra and the frenzied Ajax could be responsible in another art for the buoyant, inevitable beauty of the " Apollo Belvedere," of Mercury, " new-lit upon a heaven-kissing hill! "

Æschylus' drama displays man as an heroic figure

so long as we connect him only with the earth he treads, a pitiable child when we view him in the heaven of human experience. His drama, in spite of its conventional structure, has all the colossal lines of a frowning crag thrown up by the internal convulsions of earth, and the lyrical choruses have the splash and the motion of the sea. Sophocles refined the type, he did not alter it. He conventionalised Nemesis as an instrument useful for dramatic purposes, and possessed of this valuable stage device, he concentrated his attention on human character. This he delineated with more precision and charm than Æschylus, because his characters have deteriorated in stature. They are nearer human beings than cosmic types, and the Fate against which they too are powerless to struggle is an accident of circumstance rather than a supernatural logic. To a polite rather than a philosophic intelligence, therefore, he is more attractive. But the natural morality which, with Æschylus, sustained by its very cosmic dignity the horrors of primitive melodrama, becomes in Sophocles' hands often a trivial and unreasoned concatenation of circumstance with which the characters are not significantly connected. The tragedy is one of misfortune rather than of unreason. Moreover Sophocles' capacity for dramatic characterisation is insignificant compared with his skill in dramatic situation, upon which he almost entirely depends. He, no more than Æschylus, had looked closely into the hearts of men. Neither was to any degree a human psychologist; one was a cosmic genius, the other a fine manipulator of circumstance in the service of melodrama.

This weakness, inherent in the original conception and in the limitations of the pagan mind, becomes more and more pronounced as the later dramatist refines on the design and focusses on the smaller incident. Euripides shows more elegance of style, more sophist's cunning, more mastery of situation than the older dramatists, because he has escaped from the rude principles of Nature. He rationalises and satirises the myths. He does not tolerate and even venerate, as do his predecessors, celestial vice. At moments he humanises destiny, and even shows in his " epiphany " of the gods a realm of purer and higher virtue, of ultimate harmony above the human stage, where men and gods indulge in capricious bloodshed. But his genius was a single light that played almost sarcastically upon the prevalent darkness, condemned and discredited by his own generation, misinterpreted by those that followed. And inevitably the drama of Greece fades away into scepticism, into satire, into farce, burlesque, and silence.

If then in its origin the essential moral of Greek tragedy lay in the conflict of warring instincts, and its essential method in the magnifying of purely

natural experience, in its development the warring
instincts degenerated of necessity into petty intrigues,
and the natural experiences were dwarfed and conventionalised.   In short, it died for want of a
rational metaphysic.

This natural decay is true in a general way of
all pagan poetry as of all pagan civilisations, of
which the power fades away for lack of discretion.
It unfolds itself out of the potency of life, and
perfects itself by a progressive, though unconscious,
approximation between its matter and form and
Nature's.   This approximation could be so perfect
because pagan art mimicked Nature in human terms.
Nature often, though not always, supplied the experience, the form, and the image.   Her workmanship had only to be improved upon and displayed
to advantage.

The poetry of Christian ages had a more difficult
task, which, however, ensured it a longer survival.
Growth of mind, added to an intimidation of his
senses, had separated man from his environment,
and his effort has been increasingly directed towards
a reconciliation of his ideal desires with the recalcitrant material of his life, as that of the savage was
to adapt himself physically to his environment.
More often, therefore, his art has represented a
conflict of spirit with matter than a fusion.   At
other times the poet has been convinced of the
opposition existing between life as he would have

it and life as it is, between the world of
imaginative reason and of instinct, and he has
sought to create a world of his own in which the
processes of Nature might have no say. But in doing
so he has lost touch with the energies of life, and
his art has withered away, or at best preserved
only an attenuated existence amid dogma or didacticism. Yet the consciousness that to accept Nature
at her face value and ennoble her was not enough was
a necessary step in man's evolution, even if in the
transitional stage he tended either to impose on
Nature a personal and prejudiced philosophy, false
alike to imagination and to instinct, or denied her
creative truth and sympathy because he was incapable
as yet of discriminating her virtues and her vices
by the light of his own humanity. It was unavoidable that man's first assertion of his humanity
should represent only rebellious egotism, since he
neither understood Nature yet nor himself. For the
former he had only begun to criticise and so feared,
except when regarding her externally he worshipped
her spectacular beauty, while his own self-consciousness newly developed would tend to read itself
aggressively into all it viewed.

The poetry of ages burdened with such an effort
after knowledge is not likely to possess so generally
the external perfection evident in that of antiquity,
" ere the good and the evil wedded and begat the
best and the worst." For reason pursues the absolute,

and its infinite aim must trouble the satisfaction of the passive and pleasure-loving senses. While the pagan poet has only to be Nature's showman, the modern poet, who has learnt not only to criticise but to transcend her, is faced by the far more arduous task of reorganising the material of Nature so as to embody his more enlightened conception of beauty. He has to interpret life ideally as well as to represent it truly.

6

Yet although the needs of social life and the teaching of Christianity directed men's minds generally to a conception of life distinct from that of pagan peoples, absolute idealism was neither philosophically a discovery of the modern world nor has it been accepted as a creed of conduct in any marked degree more by modern than by ancient states. Aristotle in his *Poetics* was perhaps the first to enunciate clearly the principle that poetry is ideal in the sense that it is true to universal nature, while Plato in many passages conceives of beauty as above Nature, " eternal, unproduced, indestructible, neither subject to increase nor decay; . . . eternally uniform and consistent, and monoeidic with itself," that is, an imaginative reality as distinct from a physical moment. On the other hand, in the modern world we see only too clearly that man has not yet learnt to sublimate his savage instincts, but generally only to translate into terms of mental cunning Nature's self-interested acquisitiveness.

Yet in the general recognition of human justice as an ideal, however remote, we can admit an advance in the modern world upon the ancient. As a social animal man has slowly groped his way forward, and in the highest expression of his consciousness, in his poetry, the advance is most marked.

The most realistic poetry is removed a step from life by its medium, but in the history of our own poetry and in the biography of most of our great poets a development from sensationalism to imaginative truth can generally be traced. When a creative conception of absolute harmony, personal to the artist, discovers appropriate matter, drawn from the natural world, for its expression, we experience that pure essence of beauty in which reason and instinct unite. Such beauty is rare: indeed, much poetry which seems to satisfy our æsthetic sense on a first acquaintance for the perfect blend of its elements, grows less and less attractive as our senses tire of their pleasure and our reason seeks in vain for any idea informing the imagery. In such poetry a poet has confined himself to selecting from a mass of images certain most calculated to appeal strongly to our sensuous nature. The richer the images which he can compel into such harmony, the greater poet he is of this class. But in this process his mind is exercising a selective and not a creative discretion; it is like nature subject to life and not master of it, a mental principle inherent in a natural process rather than a creative vision expressing itself through the matter of the organic world. For Nature attains beauty by reducing her sensuous chaos to its most perfect order. Her philosophy is limited to a conviction of the value of life, which leads her often into wanton exuberance. Of spiritual values she is oblivious. She is unmoral because she is beneath humanity, not because she is above it. But the truest poet, whether he goes to life for his matter or whether he creates an imaginative world the better to express his idea, is not content merely to accept the impressions of the senses. Instead he utilises these to image his vision of a purer existence, in which the infinite desire of man for spiritual perfection is interpreted through the finite conditions under which he is compelled to live here on earth.

It is such poetry alone which is in a true sense universal. For it comprehends not only this material life where opposing forces balance each other in space, but that far subtler world of mind where ideas blend together in an indescribable harmony, that city built to music, where no physical error encroaches, and no discord lingers to be resolved.

CHAPTER III

EARLY IDEALISM IN ENGLISH POETRY

> Give me a spirit that on this life's rough sea
> Loves t' have his sails fill'd with a lusty wind,
> Even till his sail-yards tremble, his masts crack,
> And his rapt ship run on her side so low
> That she drinks water, and her keel plows air.
> There is no danger to a man that knows
> What life and death is; there's not any law
> Exceeds his knowledge; neither is it lawful
> That he should stoop to any other law.
> He goes before them, and commands them all,
> That to himself is a law rational.—CHAPMAN.

In extension the universe comprehends and engulfs me, in thought I comprehend it.—PASCAL.

I

IN the evolution of English poetry we can trace very clearly an advance from naturalism towards idealism. It is possible that the severity of their environment explains both the enlarged sense of the infinite to be found in all northern peoples and the profounder conviction of the need of moral effort. To survive at all man had to assert himself to death against the elements: to surrender to them, as was pleasant and inevitable beneath the smiling skies of the south, was very often with the northerner to perish. Our

earliest epic is in many ways more primitive than
Homer; it has less of natural grace and heroic
gesture. But its scenery is wilder, its tone more
cosmic, and its morality more intense.

Between the thunder of the sea and the desolate
mist-veiled moors and marshes, an animal people
move like shadows, more often struggling against
the brutal forces of nature, symbolised in a loath-
some monster, than enjoying the benign influences
of peace and fertility. Man is human only in his
power to direct more effectively his animal energy
so that his feats of athletic endurance may serve a
conscious end. But the end is nature's. A great
man is he who can ride the storm most stormily.
On the other hand, we find that the necessity of
rebellion against the natural forces has preserved
the northerner from deifying them as the Greeks
did. The whole distinction between modern poetry
and ancient lies in this fact, that the northerner
did not invariably bow to necessity as divine, nor
worship it as Fate.

He accepted the fact of nature's forces, and
wrestled with them. Fate, the northern goddess
" Wyrd," was to him almost what it was named
by later experience—character, and he saw as little
mere pathos in man's defeat by necessity as he
realised true sublimity in his triumph over it and
melancholy grandeur in the struggle. Where, of
course, his appetite coincided with nature's and could

be indulged without danger to himself, as a primitive man he indulged it, until in time his egotism did suffer, when he further refined upon his morality.

But against what he found to be evil to himself and possibly remediable he rebelled; he revolted against authority with all the energy of heroic egotism, when he found it grievous and cherished any hope of success. He championed free-will while admitting necessity, and the province of free-will he constantly enlarged. In short, unlike the Greeks, he imaged in the forces of life both a devil and a God, and he fought the one as fiercely as he reverenced the other. This spirit of individualism is well exemplified in the words of Brynhild in Morris's *Sigurd*.

Love thou the Gods—and withstand them, lest thy fame should
    fail in the end,
And thou be but their thrall and their bondsman, who wert born for
    their very friend.

This is the primary distinction, then, between the paganism of *Beowulf* and of Greece. In the latter there is more order, submissiveness and sunlight, in the former more of Titanic struggles and a brooding, mutinous melancholy.

By contrast how mild and genial is the world of Chaucer! The storm and darkness have given place to a mellow sunlight in which no extremes exist, and a universal charity, a kindly tolerance towards mortal weakness, presides. Chaucer's philosophy is that of uncritical humanity: he is critical only in his observance as an artist. His religion may be that of accepted dogma, but it scarcely touches his view of life at a single point. His humour has the kindness of one who has understood the frailty of all mortal things, his jests the frivolity and the genial licence of Earth herself, his pathos is sentimental, never tragic, his joy is fresh with the dew of the morning.

> But, lord Christ! when that it remembreth me
> Upon my youth, and on my jollity,
> It tickleth me about mine hearte-root,
> Unto this day it doth mine hearte boot
> That I have had my world as in my time!

When we have allowed for all the artifices and mannerisms which he took from foreign sources, this is the genius which remains, a genius which can reflect by observant sympathy every human type and embody the essential traits of each with an inspired accuracy. He records the manners of men, he does not seek to analyse their weakness or question their destiny. His is the voice of the normal good-tempered multitude who accept life for its momentary value as life, careless of its imperfections, contradictions and failures, reserving any higher conception of being to an unconsidered futurity of which religion gives us hope, but a rather vague and dreary definition, and which, therefore, they are content to leave to the theologians to quarrel over. For him:

What is this world? What asketh man to have?
Now with his love, now in his colde grave
Allone, withouten any companye.

Chaucer, then, is a poet of natural not ideal reality, content to accept the world as he finds it, and to better it not by understanding its errors, but by practising a universal forbearance. Eternity does not enter into his consideration. Time, with its momentary sunshine and shadow, is to be accepted with tolerance and good humour. If perfection there be, it must, he fancies, be in some future state of which a parson talks. It is not for man to attempt to make such perfection coincide with mortal life. And he is satisfied with presenting the human animal in its essential aspect both generic and particular. Yet even in Chaucer's writing it is easy to trace a personal development from the sensuous and fanciful affectations of his earlier translations and poems under French and Italian influence to the honest grasp of the reality of life evinced in the *Canterbury Tales.* This much his reason tutored by experience did for him, it made him true to nature. For in his handling of *Troilus and Criseyde,* having little conception of a love that transcended simple appetite, he could only superficially beautify such an appetite by dressing it in delicate imagery. Thus the beauty of the form and expression conflicting with the triviality of the matter renders the poem both psychologically false and

morally inconsistent. We love only the adorable
manner of that which we despise, and both the
treason of Criseyde, and the pathos of Troilus is
too wanton for tragedy. The *Canterbury Tales*,
however, with their earthy humour, their simple
pathos and their rank ribaldry, are a true document
of life. For here naturalism is not veiled in dainty
decoration. There is no deception practised by the
form upon the matter as in *Troilus and Criseyde*, with
its languid loveliness and affected chivalries. For
love to Chaucer was predominantly sensational:
it could be dressed in refined imagery, which may
at first deceive us into thinking it ideal, but it had no
intellectual principle beyond the generative desire
of life. The faithlessness of Criseyde no less than
the effete protestations of Troilus spring from the
innocence and the ignorance of lust. The form
only is an image of beauty, of which we can never tire.

2

The allegories and moralities of the fourteenth
and fifteenth centuries can scarcely be said to represent any growth of moral consciousness on the
part of poets. The vices and virtues which in-
trigue so confusedly throughout them are only the
personified dogmas of religion, adopted but not
naturalised by the poet, and often incongruously
obtruded upon the tangled garden of his fancy.

Allegory, with its formal machinery and its arith-
metic of virtue and of vice, is one of those systems
imposed arbitrarily upon experience, which deny
that immediate contact with life, that creative
originality, which is the essential of all true art.
The allegorist is always the pedant unless he can
transform his allegory into living symbol. He sub-
stitutes formalism for form. Such creative geniuses
as Chaucer and Spenser could fill even a borrowed
structure with life, " moral Gower " could only use
it as a pulpit. But with the Elizabethan age the
conflict between matter and mind which is sub-
sequently to be found in almost all great English
poetry for three and a half centuries clearly exists.
We see it in the dualism of the Reformation and the
Renaissance, in Protestantism on the one hand and
Paganism on the other, in the egotism of individual
poets breaking through the form and manners which
they borrowed from Italy or antiquity, in the intense
and brutal naturalism of much of the drama and
the Platonism of much of the lyric poetry, in the
naturalism of the vernacular and the learning of the
University wits, and later in the dogmatic Puritanism
into which Protestantism developed and the mannered
licence to which Renaissance grace deteriorated.
We cannot attempt here an analysis of so extensive
a period. Yet as with Elizabethan dramatists we often
find a figure of strong and rebellious moral force set
in a purely brutal and sensational environment, so

in such poets as Sidney and Spenser the dilemma of instinct and spirituality is a fundamental motif, when all allowance has been made for Platonic or allegorical affectations.

Particularly in Sidney's sonnets, the struggle between instinct which desires to possess and a suprasensuous conception of love as an emotion perfect in itself and complete in its spiritual significance is often painfully poignant. He, first of all English poets, speaks of love in purely ideal terms, yet *Astrophel and Stella* is proof that his ideal was not yet vital enough to dispute except for moments the dominance of instinct. The natural desire and its ideal sublimation exist separately in Sidney, and he alternates between their influence. In this frustrate antithesis the naked appeal of the sonnets lies, for it was never resolved. They ache with hunger unsatisfied.

Spenser unites more happily Paganism, Platonism, and Puritanism, for he gave his soul to none of them but only to Beauty: and her he worshipped first as a languid sensational goddess, but later as that essence of rational idealism, that harmonious wisdom, which he celebrates in his *Hymn to Heavenly Beauty*, exalting it alike above theology, morality, or the exquisite artifice which earlier he had cultivated. His is an early apprehension of that "Intellectual Beauty" which inspired reason abstracts from all the imagery and experience of the world, and his

pure idealism is to be found not in the system of
virtues and vices which he elaborated, while still
doubtful of true vision, in difficult and involved
allegory, not even in the perfect art with which he
reduces the manifold impressions of an avid sensibility to luxurious order, but in his later conception
of love and beauty as intellectual principles. Few
other Elizabethan lyric poets, it must be admitted,
attained to so pure a vision of either love or beauty:
but almost all combine a natural spontaneity of
song with a fancifulness and grace of form and
conceit which, though often borrowed from foreign
sources, argues at least the first stages of a critical
attitude towards instinct.

And just as in many of the dramatists, who display,
in a manner kindred to Æschylus, the insolence
of Nature entailing catastrophe, or, like Aristophanes,
her trivial licence providing farce, we find also
characters giving voice to such words of rational
determination as head this chapter, so amid much
frivolous, charming or affected song-writing we meet
also such sublime enunciations of human godhead
as Daniel's " He that of such a height hath built
his mind."

Elizabethan poetry and drama may seem predominantly to be the fruit of instinct, to reflect a natural,
at its highest a cosmic, energy, but not rarely it voices
the right of man to oppose Nature, and even exag-
gerates the virtue of rebellion. And occasionally it

rises, if only in a chance line or period, above natural to ideal reality.

Of this Shakespeare is the supreme example. As a poet, it is clear that the rich squandering of sense with which he flooded *Venus and Adonis* and *The Rape of Lucrece* with colour and music, with no ulterior aim than a realisation of material beauty, is brought " into Reason's audit " in the sonnets. Here instinct, as in Sidney, is now condemned, now avoided, but not subdued. There is in our language no more emphatic condemnation of a surrender to brute instinct in the light of imaginative reason than the sonnet " The expense of spirit in a waste of shame Is lust, in action . . ." But it is as a dramatist that his development towards absolute idealism is the most clearly revealed. From the early tragi-comedies dictated to him both by life and the fashion of the stage, from the fanciful world of love and midsummer madness, and the young fever-passion of *Romeo and Juliet*, from the buoyant wit and gentle sentiment of *As You Like It* and *Twelfth Night*, he passes on to *Hamlet, Troilus, Measure for Measure, Othello, Lear,* and *Macbeth*—the dark period of doubt and self-questioning, hard judgment and cruel sarcasm, which reveals his mind at last grappling with his instincts, condemning and scorning the animal in man and woman, and seeking painfully for a solution which will enable him to regain his lost harmony, to joy once more in the natural world without dishonouring his rational manhood. That solution is almost found in *The Winter's Tale*, it is the theme of *The Tempest*. Here indeed the opposites are reconciled; reason is relieved of responsibility; for instinct is purified of lust.

Shakespeare alone of Elizabethan dramatists felt impelled to advance from a form of poetry which presented the realities of actual life by imaging its forces in action to that in which a rarer kind of life is revealed, and warring energies, purged of their grossness, are reconciled in the conscious innocence of love. Prospero is the magician who lifts the veil from off this heavenly region and discloses it to our eyes, so that we too cry:

> O! wonder!
> How many goodly creatures are there here!
> How beauteous mankind is! O brave new world
> That has such people in it!

In Prospero surely is Shakespeare himself embodied, the Shakespeare who had experienced the sensuous self-abandonment of Romeo, the facetious melancholy of Jaques, the pathetic simplicity of Othello, the idealistic quandary of Hamlet, the tragic loneliness of Lear, and who, having drunk the gall of a sense directed world to the dregs, created out of his disillusion a celestial country where the spiritualised senses voiced the pure wisdom of love, the innocence of harmonious reason, a love so potent as a mere spectacle that it casts a spell over all discord

and closes in others the fissures of past selfishness
and lust. For in *The Tempest* all error, all sin finds
complete absolution. There is no evil left un-
appeased to generate new horrors or new strifes in
the world; even Caliban is healed of all his malice.
Elsewhere Shakespeare had created for us ideal
characters, not only true to type, such as Cleopatra, the
essential, triumphant embodiment of natural womanhood, or Othello, the gigantic, pathetic pattern of
natural man, but also ideal in absolute virtue and
beauty, whether of Perdita, the peerless maid, or
Imogen, the perfect wife. Yet even in *The Winter's
Tale* the thought of Mamillius dead in his childish
innocence lingers to haunt our minds with the sense
of error and passion and all its pains. But in *The
Tempest* the ideal qualities defeated in the tragedies
either through some subtle weakness in the pos-
sessor of them or by the conspiracy of physical
circumstance not only survive in full self-realisa-
tion, but also convert by their spirituality the very
material world which would naturally deny and
destroy them.

To present this triumph of ideal over natural
values Shakespeare was compelled to have recourse
to fantasy. Such a world might, indeed, seem attainable only by miraculous means, and yet Prospero's
magic is only the enlightened reason which appears
supernatural to the savage mind. Ariel's wings are
but the wings of unfettered spirit which ranges

joyously over the grosser matter of life and shapes it to its purpose. Caliban, " this thing of darkness," is Nature in her unreasoning lewdness ruling a human form and stamping it with the features of the brute. It was left for a later generation to relate essential values to life as it is. Shakespeare pre-eminently among Elizabethan dramatists at last realised the values in himself, attaining thereby agreement among his faculties and peace in his soul, and creating in *The Tempest* a new and supernatural world to express them.

In so far, however, as naturalism predominated even in the egotism of the Elizabethan age, periods of precocious growth and decadence were inevitable. The drama inaugurated by Marlowe and perfected by Shakespeare retained its primitive force in the great moments of Webster, Tourneur and Ford, but it faded away into the agreeable cleverness of Fletcher, the dramatic ingenuity of Massinger, and the false sentiment of Shirley. As the mystical paganism of Æschylus ends in the licence and satire of Aristophanes, so the physical arrogance of the early Elizabethans and their passionate sensibility towards life leaves as its immediate posterity the ribald humours of Congreve and Wycherley. Yet, as we have already stated, such ebbing and flowing as we see in English literature is not final; it is rather like the ripples running backwards and forwards on the surface of an ever advancing tide.

The evolution of our literature as a whole is from
sensationalism to natural idealism, and from natural
to creative idealism. Superficially this continuous
movement towards a higher and profounder conception of life, truth, and beauty is made up of
periodical advances and retrogressions through an
exaggeration by one generation either of the sensational or the rational element in consciousness,
which entails an equally exaggerated reaction in the
generation which follows. Thus after the untempered
surrender by the Elizabethans to an instinctive love
of life, to physical self-assertion and animal aggrandisement, there followed an age which condemned
life as savagely as its predecessor had applauded it.

In the earlier age, of the two influences which we
have named, an arrogant paganism was more powerful
than a critical Protestantism, flamboyant nature
than determining reason, in that which followed
the position was reversed. The pagan element had
gradually lost its energy, at the same time shedding
its affected Platonism, and had degenerated into
feeble licence, but the unformulated Protestantism
had developed into a vigorous Puritanism which
asserted a moral egotism with all the force and
narrowness of Nature. The very timidity of the
Puritan augmented his individualism. For, fearing
to surrender his instinct to Nature, he compelled her
force into the bigoted service of his mind. Thus the
age which succeeds to Shakespeare proclaims the

passing of pagan gaiety and the coming of moral fear. And from fear came hardness of mind and narrowness of sympathy, and eventually the defeat of poetry by dogma. To state it in another way, we may say that for English poetry, the age of feudalism, of Latinism, and of aristocracy, died with Spenser. The poetry which accepted the licence and passion of life as its uncriticised content, and refined upon it only in the form of its presentation, in the technical grace of art, without questioning its truth, was superseded. Nature had exhausted her energy for a time, and religion had woken to the catastrophes that ensued in life from a servile surrender to instinct. And because it did not understand the nature of Beauty, and could not discriminate between a vulgar satisfaction of desire and an imaginative rendering of sensuous experience, it bid men distrust life's impulse altogether. It visioned virtue not in nature truly discriminated, but rather in life denied, creating a negative morality and substituting for the passion of wise living the dead letter of an angry law.

This morality has by many writers been condemned. In itself it deserves many of their strictures. Yet it served a necessary purpose without which neither poetry nor civilisation could have made much advance. The main stream of Elizabethan energy was democratic, and it was rude and uncouth as all young democracies are. The paganism, therefore, which had been so sifted by the educated minds of Italian writers that only a delicate sensationalism, sometimes vicious, sometimes falsely sublime, remained, impelled many English poets, little educated by learning or experience, into brutal excess and discord. The old wine went to the heads of a young people unused to drinking, and an alien paganism combined forcefully with an indigenous naturalism, which was uncontrolled, as in older civilisations, by any tradition of art. And although such Elizabethans as Sidney and Spenser were sufficiently educated in the language and thought of the Renaissance to reflect all the refinements of another civilisation together with a native honesty, the secret of that exquisite sensuousness, the last direct echo of classical times, was bound to die with them in the turmoil of increasingly modern and material conditions.

Religion, which knew little of art, was not ignorant of life, and the negative morality which it inculcated, even if its principles were narrow and its methods savage, aimed at convincing man of the need to control the forces apt to be rampant in any young and healthy organism. It taught men to deny nature for the time, that they might return to her armed with principles which would enable them to use her to their own honour, and to that of art and of life.

CHAPTER IV

IDEALISM AND PURITANISM

To touch the heart of his mystery, we find in him the thought of Duty; the thought of something owing to himself, to his neighbour, to his God.—R. L. STEVENSON.

I

MILTON on a large canvas, Donne on a small, illustrate the conflict of Paganism and Protestantism; such mystical poets as Vaughan, Herbert, or Traherne, a first attempt to reconcile a natural ecstasy with Christian devotion. Milton to some extent unites in himself the Renaissance and the Reformation, a creative age and a critical, a worship of vital beauty and of absolute law, of God's sunlight and of God's judgment. The two are not contraries, as has so often been said, but consequences. The worship of life grew naturally into the service of God, the love of the finite and visible world into the quest of the infinite and invisible, as reason pierced deeper into experience.

Milton was born too late to surrender to the intoxication of life, even in youth, as completely as the poets of the creative age, which immediately preceded him. His earlier poems reflect the grace and artifice, but not the wantonness, of the Renaissance. Even in their revelry they are artistically austere, while in his *Hymn to the Nativity*, religious fervour speaks with that purity and gaiety of natural innocence, which, except in the so-called metaphysical poets, was never again to be attained until Puritan zeal eventually exhausted itself. Life was to Milton in his young day as it was to Adam and Eve on that memorable evening in Eden:

> With thee conversing, I forget all time,
> All seasons, and their change; all please alike.
> Sweet is the breath of Morn, her rising sweet,
> With charm of earliest birds; pleasant the sun,
> When first on this delightful land he spreads
> His orient beams, on herb, tree, fruit and flower,
> Glistering with dew; fragrant the fertile earth
> After soft showers; and sweet the coming on
> Of grateful Evening mild; then silent Night,
> With this her solemn bird, and this fair Moon,
> And these the gems of Heaven, her starry train.

But in him, as in all great creative genius, we see the same advance, partial and imperfect though it was, towards truth, which the genius of humanity at large has pursued so slowly by comparison, and is still pursuing.

The plucking of the fruit of knowledge exiled him, no less than Adam and Eve, from his early Paradise. *Paradise Lost* is an epic of its author's spiritual history as well as of man's. The religion of the senses is enchanting in youth, but disaster dogs its indulgence, and so impels a poet to examine rationally his experience. It teaches him first to dread life and either to withdraw from contact with her or to rear between himself and her the barrier of moral law, at best an imperfect method of avoiding nature's excesses, at worst a summary denial of life's fairest expressions. Milton's cultivation of human and personal values, of morality in any real sense, did not go very far. For he was considerably more mediæval than he was critical, and so, except where such interested motives as a recalcitrant wife, or political partisanship, dictated a liberal and individual standpoint, he was, with all his repetition of religious dogma and scriptural myths, predominantly pagan. Only very occasionally can he be said even to harmonise the Renaissance and the Reformation. He is a humanist merely in the pomp of his learning and no more than a Political Protestant. Certainly life placed the orthodox despot in awkward predicaments, and forced him against his will to adopt the rôle of the rebel. The mediæval anti-feminist is also the impassioned pleader for divorce; the loyal prophet of a Calvinistic God is also the sympathetic creator of a Satan who is the noblest free-thinker in our literature; the biblical dramatist of Samson preaches the exultant ethic of a Greek tragedian. But the reason is that he had a personal interest in furthering divorce, in drawing rebellion heroically, and in blackening a Dalila.

But fundamentally Milton was a pagan, troubled

with a Puritan conscience. Behind his moral announcements, the ethics of savagery are often only too apparent. He denies life as a Puritan with the same brutality with which a pagan accepted it. And indeed much Puritanism is manifestly only an inverse form of sensuality, a savage negation of pleasure essentially kindred to a brutal indulgence.

Yet though *Paradise Lost* signifies the first expression of a narrowly Puritan conscience by a poet, Milton loved life so lavishly that he could, as an artist, turn a negative doctrine into a positive faith. Puritanism, however, entails a surrender of the poet's ultimate right, by prejudging life. For the poet should welcome ardently all experiences, raising them to a plane of spiritual significance by his inspired sense of values. Milton's acceptance of doctrine does often compromise his poetry, and would have confined his epic to the province of mechanical logic and tribal law, had not his majestic apprehension of natural beauty compelled him to build a luxurious world over a desert of dogma.

Puritanism, which killed in England the poetry of life, which became in its very hatred and fear of the senses often more brutal than the senses themselves, could never subdue in Milton the Renaissance passion for plastic beauty. It provided *Paradise Lost* with a biblical structure over which a sumptuous and self-sufficient imagery could spread itself, and in *Samson Agonistes* it fused with a latent paganism

to produce a drama as primitive in its sublime
exultation over revenge as any drama of Æschylus.
In Milton therefore, as in Dante, the ideas of
paganism and Christianity are inextricably confused,
and the devil of *Paradise Lost*, the principle of
satanic vitality, is little inferior as a moral being to
God, the symbol of vengeful justice. Milton reveals
reason, in short, developed only to the point of
disputing with the senses without transcending their
principle. His morality was as physical in its condemnation of sin as sensation had been in its acceptance of life. His idealism was absolute only in the
high imaginative moments when reason and sensation combined to transcend each other's limitations.

Yet Puritanism, in its dread of the "wanton
stings and motions of the sense," in its anxiety to
keep virtue unsquandered by improvident vice,
in its accurate judgment of man's moral weakness,
and lastly in its very inability to diagnose life, and
so suggest a remedy by which human nature could
heal itself, was bound to preach a denial of nature,
as the necessary prelude to rational control. Such
a denial was the temporary expedient of ignorance.
And it is a misfortune that the negative attitude of
Puritanism, the emphasis which it laid on the sup-
pression of vice rather than the development of
virtue, has depressed English life and thought, if
we except one brief and too hasty revolt, almost to
our own day. Only recently has it received its

death-blow at the hands of Science, which by dis-
closing to man the machinery of nature has begun
to free his mind from superstition and fear.

Puritanism, however, only gradually encroached
upon the instinctive idealism of poetry, which, after
destroying, it was to revive more truly later. For the
poet has his own vision, which must always in some
degree transcend the temporary compromises of
conventional religion. And since Puritanism, before
it hardened into dogma, was a conception which
man had evolved for himself out of his experience
of error, it possessed at first a vital and personal
significance. Much of the sensuousness of Chaucer
and the early Elizabethans was native, but much
was reflected at second-hand from a more luxurious
civilisation, and by a class too, which, in the growth
of society, had risen above the level of toiling sub-
sistence, and was sheltered in court or university.
Puritanism restored the ancient feud between man
and nature, which was part of his race instinct, but
substituted the impulses of his own personal instinct
for the world of inanimate nature, as the force which
it was his manhood's duty to quell.

In the poetry therefore which reflects Puritanism,
not as a dogma, but as a personal attitude towards
life, we should expect to find two new qualities,—an
analysis of sensation in place of a pure surrender to
it, and an attempt to create a perfect world rather than
accept the vicarious pleasures of the world as it is.

Puritanism urged that instinct was vicious, and the poet whose sensibility renders him particularly prone to the appeal of pleasure, whose purest vision is based upon instinct, was likely at first not to refuse the allurements of nature, but after surrendering himself to them, to examine his experience in the aftermath of disgusted satiety, and thence to evolve certain moral values. Such a one was Donne. Others with natures less rooted in material life, would be persuaded by the strictures of Puritanism to turn their eyes away from an existence where all seemed shifting squalor, seeking out some region of heavenly calm, some far province or natural Paradise Regained to which only the soul could travel, and where the body could not trouble with its discord, nor passion lead to error, injury, disgust or regret. Of such a quality is the poetry of Herbert and Vaughan, of Crashaw and Traherne.

2

In Donne, however, we meet a being rich alike in reason and in instinct, and the two elements are ever in fierce conflict. In his youth he sought passionately every carnal experience, in his age he pursued no less avidly the questionings of the mind. Curiosity was vital in him. We are inclined to ask his ever restless temperament

> Is not thy sacred hunger of science
> Yet satisfied?

In his early years he viewed the satisfaction or frustration of frankly physical desires in cynical retrospect. He took pleasure and then mocked himself for his indulgence, and the object of his pleasure for its faithless transience. His love was based in the physical, was indeed at times so earthy, that it could express itself in such a poem as the *Flea*, yet it was not animal because it was consciously physical. Donne admitted and intellectualised his lust with a refreshing honesty, which led in the end to a clear mental definition of the limitations of the body and the requirements of the spirit, and at its most inspired to an expression of the spirit through the body:

> Her pure and eloquent blood
> Spoke in her cheeks and so distinctly wrought
> That one might almost say her body thought.

Donne, then, never sentimentalised an instinct or shirked the humiliating admission of animality. His epithalamia and such elegies as *To His Mistress going to Bed*, are a celebration of all that is purely sensuous in marriage, are frank naturalism, accepted with exultancy. Yet his mind is for ever sneering at both the tyranny and transiency of purely physical pleasure.

> He is stark mad, whoever says
> That he hath been in love an hour,
> Yet not that love so soon decays,
> But that it can ten in less space devour;

> Who will believe me if I swear
> That I have had the plague a year?
> Who would not laugh at me, if I should say
> I saw a flash of powder burn a day?

Yet later he came to realise in the sensation of love, physically so momentary, the one changeless reality in the whirl of time.

> All kings, and all their favourites,
> All glory of honours, beauties, wits,
> The sun itself, which makes time, as they pass,
> Is elder by a year now than it was
> When thou and I first one another saw.
> All other things to their destruction draw,
> Only our love hath no decay;
> This no to-morrow hath, nor yesterday.
> Running it never runs from us away,
> But truly keeps his first, last, everlasting day.

And from a perception of Love as expressing out of "the dead thing" which he felt himself to be

> A quintessence even from nothingness,

he advanced to that psychical apprehension of the soul as a thing distinct from the body and yet expressed through it, which he embodied in *The Ecstasy*.

> As, 'twixt two equal armies, Fate
> Suspends uncertain victory,
> Our souls—which to advance their state
> Were gone out—hung 'twixt her and me.
>
> And whilst our souls negotiate there,
> We like sepulchral statues lay,
> All day, the same our postures were,
> And we said nothing, all the day.

· · · ·

This ecstasy doth unperplex
(We said) and tell us what we love;
We see by this, it was not sex;
We see, we saw not, what did move:

.   .   .   .

But O alas! so long, so far,
Our bodies why do we forbear?
They are ours, though not we; we are
Th' intelligences, they the spheres.

We owe them thanks, because they thus
Did us to us, at first, convey,
Yielded their senses' force to us,
Nor are dross to us, but allay.

.   .   .   .

As our blood labours to beget
Spirits, as like souls as it can;
Because such fingers need to knit
That subtle knot, which makes us man;

So must pure lovers' souls descend
To affections, and to faculties,
Which sense may reach and apprehend,
Else a great prince in prison lies.

To our bodies turn we then, that so
Weak men on love reveal'd may look;
Love's mysteries in souls do grow
But yet the body is his book.

We have quoted so much of this poem because it
is perhaps the subtlest spiritual interpretation of the
senses which this age achieved.   An individual
genius accomplished it; the mind and instinct of the
age fell far short of any such conception, and poetry,
as we shall see, for long either avoided the material

problem by escaping to an abstract ideal, or turned the physical to the uses of wit or of appetite. Donne loved the physical with all the healthy relish of Elizabethan youth, but as his Puritan conscience forbade him to rest satisfied with the rewards of the body, so his love of life assured him of a reality beyond the bounds of logic. He combined the lust of the brute, the curiosity of the scientist and the aspirations of the saint, and as the heat of youth cooled, the latter two qualities predominated over the former, upon the memory of which, however, they drew for experience. As we know, he took orders, became Dean of St. Paul's and disowned his earlier verse, while the mental cunning with which he had dissected his appetite went into light satire, his yearning for eternal principles into a form of devout philosophy.

" Reason is our soul's left hand, faith her right," so he cried, and in his great analysis of the divine part in man in *The Progress of the Soul* he cross-examines sensuality with a patient rather than a caustic tongue. In brief his conclusions are that " Nature hath no gaol, though she hath law," and " The only measure is, and judge, opinion,"—surely as enlightened a perception both of the limits of the natural world, and the responsibility of human reason, as ever enunciated. No poet has seen more clearly into the truth of nature than Donne, although many have sung of her more splendidly. He had great difficulty in reconciling the fact and the idea, or rather in attaining that exact balance between instinct and intelligence by which spiritual vision is attained, and this doubtless explains the almost invariable strain and tautness both of his images and his rhythm. The soul and body in human love, this earth and eternity in religious faith, are with him constantly in conflict, only rarely do they coincide.

> I am a little world made cunningly
> Of elements, and an angelic sprite;
> But black sin hath betray'd to endless night
> My world's both parts, and, O, both parts must die.

And this, possibly more than disease and fasting, accounts for the physical horror with which in his last years he viewed the approach of death. And yet

> One short sleepe past, wee wake eternally,
> And death shall be no more; death thou shalt die.

His morbid fear of the winding-sheet and the worm was but the last protest of that flesh which had taken such early relish in a carnal life.

3

The mystical poets (for those to whom we shall refer here are better described as mystical than metaphysical) were devotional as Donne in his later years, yet not through self-discipline, but with all the immediate conviction of inexperienced childhood. Theirs is the innocence, the rapture of pure natures, which have escaped any strong temptation either to earthliness or to knowledge. That childlike apprehension of a heavenly Paradise, which is, as it were, imposed on the realm of nature and of man, so that all their crudities and cruelties are consumed in a pure wonder at life's essential miracle, is native to all of them. It is as if they saw the earth only in the first hour of sunrise, with the dew still fresh upon it, and never lived to know the foul deeds that were done in the heat of noon, or the squalor that the night concealed. They have, in short, all the vision and blindness of saintliness. The degree, however, of mysticism in these poets varied. In many a conviction of the unity underlying all things was languid and superficial. It led only to the forced wedding of remote opposites in simile and metaphor, as if in a conscious attempt to advertise the relationship of far-sundered particulars. Many of the " ingenious devices " and fantastic affectations of Cowley and his school are of this order. And even from the religious poets a passionate personal vision is often absent. Both Crashaw and Herbert more often improvise intricately on conventional themes or scriptural formulas than express their " Flaming Hearts," as Crashaw can, for example, in his "Nativity Hymn," entangling the Saviour whom he addresses in an inspired naturalism,—

> We saw Thee in Thy balmy nest,
> Bright Dawn of our eternal Day!

We saw Thine eyes break from their east
  And chase the trembling shades away.
We saw Thee, and we blest the sight.
We saw Thee by Thine own sweet light.

Vaughan too can only imitate Herbert or air a correct devotion or a pious meditation, save in those moments of pure ecstasy, when he outstrips all rivals, and encircles his verse in "a ring of pure and endless light," while Traherne, in his poetry, is more mystical in attempt than in attainment. Yet possibly it is his prose *Meditations* which express these poets' mystical innocence, their state of ecstatic naturalism at its best; as he tells of

Those pure and virgin apprehensions I had in my infancy, and that divine light wherewith I was born.

All appeared new at first, inexpressibly rare and delightful and beautiful. I was a little stranger which at my entrance into the world was saluted and surrounded with innumerable joys. My knowledge was Divine.... I seemed as one brought into the estate of innocence. All things were spotless and pure and glorious; yea, and infinitely mine and joyful and precious. I knew not that there were any sins, or complaints or laws. I dreamed not of poverties, contentions or vices. All tears and quarrels were hidden from mine eyes. Everything was all rest, free and immortal.

Or again:

The corn was orient and immortal wheat which never should be reaped nor ever was sown. I thought it had stood from everlasting to everlasting. . . . Boys and girls tumbling in the street were moving jewels. I knew not that they were born or should die. But all things bided eternally as they were in their proper places. Eternity was manifest in the Light of the Day, and something infinite behind everything appeared, which talked with my expectation and moved my desire.

Or again:

My soul was only apt and disposed to great things; but souls to souls are like apples, one being rotten rots another. ·

And later:

Being swallowed up therefore in the miserable gulf of idle talk and worthless vanities, thenceforth I lived among shadows, like a prodigal son feeding upon husks with swine. A comfortless wilderness full of thorns and troubles the world was or worse; a waste place covered with idleness and play, and shops, and markets, and taverns. . . . So that I had wholly forgotten all goodness, bounty, comfort and glory. . . . Sometimes I should soar above the stars, and inquire how the Heavens ended, and what was beyond them.

And lastly:

When I heard of any new kingdom beyond the seas, the light and glory of it entered into me, it rose up within me, and I was enlarged wonderfully. I entered into it.

It was as if here the adventurous spirit of the Elizabethans had been suddenly sublimated, had become a pursuit of ideal fantasy, in which these poets are pioneers, questing after some region made after the spirit of nature, but not the letter.

Yet in " these liquid clear satisfactions " which Traherne considered " the emanations of the highest reason " we find invariably what we may call the limitation of the infinite. We see first the blissful satisfaction of the young creature who finds himself in exact accord with the vital impulses of nature.

He is a nerve of that great body of the earth, and he vibrates in human but unconscious sympathy with the stream and the grass and the stars; and where he comes into contact with the work of man, true again to nature he spreads over it a self-created vegetation sprung from his own fancy. In short, he sentimentalises reality to satisfy his own desire; "The dust and stones of the street were as precious as gold," he writes. "I was a weak and little child and had forgotten there was a man alive in the earth." It is a convenient obliviousness.

Man and his works do not yet exist in so primitive a consciousness absorbed and lost to definition in mystical rapture. Indeed we might well trace in such beings, as we see in rare childhood, a return to pre-social conditions of life, albeit with natures divinely spiritualised, miraculously purged, of all the savagery inherent in a state of nature. But as the mind of such poets develops, the facts of life begin to assert themselves, and with a shock corresponding to the intensity of that early paradisal vision. We can fancy that so the spirit of Nature herself must have trembled as she viewed the first industrial town shaping into hideousness.

The world becomes a "comfortless wilderness full of thorns and troubles." So it appeared to these poets obsessed still with the glory of their young, unclouded morning. Can we wonder that they flinched, that they avoided the grim, the tragic contrast between the harmony of nature's balance of power, felt in the blood and refined by the mind into a supernatural conception,—and man's first brutal efforts to create a world of human order? That joyous principle of life, they, blind to its ruthless methods in the physical world, had fashioned into a vision of enraptured, harmonious experience. It was this that they named Eternity, and for them " All time was Eternity, and a perpetual Sabbath." That identity which they felt with life, that sense of comprising in themselves the Heavens and the Earth, so that the distinction between the two faded, and the kingdom of heaven was verily within and around them, was what they meant by sonship, and what they worshipped as God.

It is not for us to question their disregard of fact. It is enough to remark upon it. The life around them they found in their moments of consciousness to be " nasty, brutish, and mean," the temporary result, had they known it, of a compromise between the impulses of nature and an imperfect exercise of human will. They disregarded it, for they found in it discord, unhappiness and death. In nature, had they looked candidly, they would have found the same, but they would have found it only after piercing below the veil of general beauty to the particular ugliness, only after submitting the principle of life, successful in its large results, to the scrutiny of a mind in which not one sparrow may perish

I

unconsidered. Nature is most pure an artist in the large and in the small, in the landscape and the leaf. It is in the intermediate regions between these that her licence is discovered, her creative excess multiplying matter in formless decoration, and destroying it in confused decay. With these facts it was not for them to wrestle. It is music's, as it is poetry's, function to resolve discord, but it may choose its own province, whether it be that of its own troubled or joyous heart or the heart of imperfect mankind, or the heart of eternity, is a matter for its own discretion, provided only it tell sincerely of each. Its success, whatever its province, may be judged from the degree of reality and harmony which it can express through its chosen medium. Meredith wrestled with the world of human and natural values, as an intellectual giant, and his language is full of the stress and irritation of the struggle. Vaughan, responding only to those superhuman values which were in him an idealisation of the creative ecstasy of nature, a state in which all nature's perpetual change and her ephemeral moments are concentrated into one unalterable moment at the essential, trembling core of existence, cries:

> I saw Eternity, the other night,
> Like a great Ring of pure and endless light,
> All calm as it was bright;
> And round beneath it, Time, in hours, days, years,
> Driv'n by the spheres,
> Like a vast shadow mov'd.

How the poetic faculty gives body to what is after
all a pure abstraction, an aura glittering in a heavenly
haze, is well illustrated by this other well-known
poem of his, which bodies a vague transcendentalism
in the figure of Christ himself:

> My soul, there is a country
> Far beyond the stars,
> Where stands a winged sentry
> All skilful in the wars:
>
> There above noise and danger,
> Sweet Peace sits crowned with smiles,
> And one born in a manger
> Commands the beauteous files.
>
> He is thy gracious Friend,
> And—O my soul, awake!—
> Did in pure love descend
> To die here for thy sake.
>
> If thou canst get but thither,
> There grows the flower of Peace,
> The Rose, that cannot wither,
> Thy fortress, and thy ease.
>
> Leave then thy foolish ranges;
> For none can thee secure
> But One who never changes—
> Thy God, thy life, thy cure.

In Herbert the sense of eternity, of infinite existence,
is translated from a vision into a principle, that of
Love. The translation is direct and logical. He who
loves the Infinite loves every embodiment of it
which he presupposes in the Finite. He does not
criticise the Finite, or venture the opinion that in

this creature the Infinite is less apparent than in that. He sees the Infinite in all things, and loves accordingly.

> I cannot ope mine eyes,
> But Thou art ready there to catch
> My morning soul and sacrifice.

And:

> Teach me Thy love to know:
> That this new light, which now I see,
> May both the work and workman show.

That light was not the light of reason, but the light " that never was, on sea or land," a light cast directly by the human aspiring and creative soul over the darkness of actuality, which it denied and disregarded, a romantic radiance not drawn out of the world as it was, but distilled (as it were) out of the joyous experience of the human senses, vibrating in sympathy with life. Both pure joy and brutal sensualism are " beyond good and evil," because they represent a surrender of consciousness to the creative impulse, and the distinction between them lies in the quality of that surrender. The desire of the sensualist is material: he desires physical satisfaction, material possession, at all costs, and he takes no thought for its quality or its consequences. He disregards his humanity and embodies the principle of nature, although moving in what should be a world of more sensitive values. Thus he disgraces his manhood by surrendering and even exploiting rationally the instinct which he shares with the brutes. He destroys his own patents of nobility. But the Love of which Herbert sings is as uncritical in its inspiration as common lust is in its impulse. The difference is one of quality, of which the one is spiritual, the other physical; the one seeks only heavy increase of itself (at the cost, if necessary, of another), the other, an identification of the soul, of the essential being with that universal life in which spiritually we move and have our being. The one demands a self-gratification which is only increased because rendered more conscious, if it entail a certain savage struggle for mastery, the other a harmony in which the internal harmony of the individual merges itself in the wider harmony of the whole. The physical senses imprison a man in himself, but the aim of spiritualised instinct is to experience the essential rhythm of life. In such a being the desires of manhood cannot supplant the purity of childhood, but only enrich it. " His soul is yet a white paper unscribbled with observations of the world, wherewith at length it becomes a blurred notebook. He is purely happy because he knows no evil, nor hath made means by sin to be acquainted with misery. He arrives not at the mischief of becoming wise, nor endures evils to come by foreseeing them."

And the transiency of so much poetry based on the senses, and unconnected with any higher principle of thought or feeling, the expression as it is of love snatched with the swift desperation of the thief, and lost as soon as won, is in these poets transformed into that intuition of eternity which is an ever-lasting moment, and in which all moments are contained. So Herbert tells of it:

> I got me flowers to strew Thy way;
> I got me boughs off many a tree;
> But Thou wast up by break of day
> And brought'st Thy sweets along with Thee.
>
> The sun arising in the East,
> Though he give light, and the East perfume,
> If they should offer to contest
> With Thy arising, they presume.
>
> Can there be any day but this,
> Though many suns to shine endeavour?
> We count three hundred, but we miss:
> There is but one, and that one ever.

And thus Crashaw:

> Lord, when the sense of Thy sweet grace
> Sends up my soul to seek Thy face,
> Thy blessed Eyes breed such desire
> I die in love's delicious fire.
>
> O Love! I am thy sacrifice,
> Be still triumphant, blessed eyes:
> Still shine on me, fair sun, that I
> Still may behold, though still I die.
>
> Though still I die, I live again,
> Still longing so to be still slain;
> So gainful is such loss of breath,
> I die even in desire of Death.

> Still live in me this loving strife
> Of living death and dying life:
> For while Thou sweetly slayest me,
> Dead to myself, I live in Thee.

Such ecstasy we would scarcely connect with Puritanism, and yet to Puritanism we owe it. In these poets the moral or rational principle for which Puritanism stood had not yet descended to negative criticism. It was absorbed into an act of sensuous refinement, into a sublimation of instinct, until it became intuition. It had not begun to judge or to deny life, only to transcend it. Sin touched these poets delicately; they escaped the self by ecstasy and not by chastisement, so that evil and pain never embittered their faith nor clouded their joyousness. They knew sin for what it was, but in the sunlight of their pure natures they consumed its darkness; they sought their habitation in the heaven of their inward light. At the most, in moments of dejection these children of light exchanged an immediate rapture for a rapture of reminiscence, as in Vaughan's *Retreat*:

> Happy those early days, when I
> Shin'd in my angel-infancy!
> Before I understood this place
> Appointed for my second race;
> Or taught my soul to fancy aught
> But a white, celestial thought; . . .
>
> O how I long to travel back,
> And tread again that ancient track!
> That I might once more reach that plain,
> Where first I left my glorious train.

And if we must add a word of criticism to an appreciation of their spiritual spontaneity, it is that in their own pure ecstasy that "felt through all this fleshly dress Bright shoots of everlastingness," they left mankind rather forlorn. The escape answered for them; for their natures were but little stained with the soil of this world. But for those who still struggled through the loam of earth with how faint and inconstant a perception of any tranquil heaven (and of such were the majority of their age, and for that matter, of our own), this blissful idealism, that sang of God and eternity, as the lark lost in the sky's immensity, could bring but small comfort and doubtful persuasion. In the white light of their ecstasy, the colours of life, no less than the shadows and the soil upon its features, are burnt up.

The saint offers perhaps a less convincing parable to humanity than the sinner striving after virtue. Men needed not so much an idealisation of the inanimate universe as a cry straight from the human heart, tortured by its own infamy and struggling towards better things. Mankind was still too dangerously natural to pay heed to, or profit by, the supernatural. And these mystical poets did not understand the facts of nature; they loved pure life passionately, and they worshipped it in self-forgetful ecstasy as a God in whose person eternity dwelt. Their idealism did not grow out of the labour and the disillusionment of human life;

but they avoided in their pure enthusiasm that more arduous task of reconciling the problem of human life in all its naked realism with their divine ideal. They forgot the needs of earth because the stars amazed them. And yet as mankind advances towards a higher conception of his purpose and a clearer recognition of his needs, the mysticism of these poets will more and more partake of common day-light. Their spiritual valuation, which saw in time only eternity, in love only self-forgetful harmony, in nature only the triumphant beauty of the creative impulse (and that so vividly that her destructiveness was hid from their eyes), will surely in the end co-incide with human principles. It does not now, and it did not then. For men had passed from their first childhood, and it will be long before they enter into their second.

For the time, in Traherne's words, man lives " among shadows, like a prodigal son, feeding upon husks with swine." And though he needs the light, it must not beckon to him from too great a distance. The stars cannot pierce through the smoke and flame that veil the battlefield. Only the fearless sun that searches the dark places of this earth can pene-trate the murk of that grim warfare, in which the forces of nature and of reason strive desperately for the mastery.

The mystical poets won to a perception of perfect values, by sympathising with all that is beautiful and positive in nature, and by shutting their eyes to all that is ugly and negative. They purged sensualism of its grossness, and built a visionary heaven upon a visionary earth. And because earth in its actuality is inviting and imminent, and heaven speculative and a little cold, their ecstasy remained a curious and unique occurrence in the onward march of poetry. It has been debased by the composers of hymns, it has given many a religious soul comfort and satisfaction; over the development of poetry itself, over the consciousness of even educated men, it has exercised but little influence. Not until the end of the nineteenth century was the same tone of religious ecstasy to be enriched by the "still sad music of humanity" in the person of one who had suffered as an outcast, and walked the pavements of the world in want—by Francis Thompson.

4

Finally, to summarise briefly the quality of later and less purely devotional verse in the seventeenth century, we may say that we find the natural idealism of the Elizabethans, in the spirit of which they sang their "native wood-notes wild," with as blithe an instinct as ever did bird upon a May morning, however derivative at times their form, broken up by the first intrusions of critical thought. The main pathways, if we may so term them, of emotion had been traversed.   Men were now seeking truth in the by-paths.   For even outside the devotional verse of such poets as Quarles, Sandys, Crashaw, Vaughan or Herbert, Puritanism was a powerful factor, leading many to reject the classical manner, the external naturalism of paganism, as sharing in the odium now so generally cast upon all earthly vanities.   In place of objective symbols borrowed from nature, Puritanism was trying to discover and create for itself new, individual and sometimes abstruse symbols, which might convey its own intimate consciousness of a divinity immanent in life, but closely akin to human reason.   Doubtless often the far-fetched conceits which these poets use are the outcome of conscious ingenuity and serve the ends of manufactured surprise.   No longer does passion, as with the Elizabethans, bear them buoyantly on its stream, no longer does an inevitable heightening of emotion demand the extraordinary in a fine excess.   And for this reason the angle at which they observed life is very similar to that of to-day.   We share with them a reaction from a strong and confident creative period to one of more scrupulous questioning and more complicated states of mind.   The generality and the instinctive dogma has been superseded by particular observance and intellectual subtlety.   Science in short is mingled with sentiment.

Even so in the seventeenth century we find that

the idealism of many poets is become fragmentary, but exact, in place of organic and general. They draw nice distinctions. Yet their view of life is not yet materialised; rather is their sense of the infinite intensified by being rendered more conscious. Instead of merely feeling, they also think; instead of singing, they see with a close observance of the facts which interpose between them and the eternal universe of freedom which they seek. As Alexander Browne wrote:

> The glories of your ladies be
> But metaphor of things.

All the details of life—even the flower and the sparrow—were become to them symbols of eternity. Behind the most trivial verse of the time lurks this ardent, often mournful, and sometimes ironic mysticism. It is found in their most candid and detached celebrations of the physical, even in such a poem as Carew's *Rapture*, and in the countless epitaphs or elegies in which they do honour to the dead. As in Sir Thomas Browne's *Evening Hymn*:

> Sleep is death. Oh! make me try
> By sleeping what it is to die.
> And as gently lay my head
> On my grave, as now my bed.

And:

> Oh! come that hour when I shall never
> Sleep again, but wake for ever.

Or again, in Cowley's:

> Then down I laid my head,
> Down on cold earth, and for a while was dead,
> And my freed soul to a strange somewhere fled.

No longer the unquestioning children of life, they were still free from the morbid fear either of sensuous pleasure or of personal extinction, which marks a later decadence.

But love and life and death were to them states to be, as it were, explored and exploited, to be scanned cunningly for confirmation of their own still insatiable greed for vitality.

> Grief is a puddle, and reflects not clear
> Your beauty's rays,

wrote Carew; and all life was a stream out of the transparency or opacity of which these poets sought to draw significant reflections. Their moods had no longer the simple spontaneity of the Elizabethans; both in the physical and emotional spheres their minds had begun to create subtleties, to criticise and to refine, yet still with a general intuition of the organic note of an universal life, of which their own experiences were the rippling variations.

Amid therefore much conscious eroticism, realism, and artificial conceit, we almost always feel that this ardent pursuit of the infinite in the particular, and the strained metaphors and epithets which from the time of Johnson have been so cursorily condemned in the school of Cowley, the exaggerations which Pope set himself to rectify, are the inevitable result of an attempt on their part to record precisely infinite experiences, which were also intimately personal. Unfortunately for the interpretation of these particular, individual and ideal emotions, they tried to utilise forms fashioned to convey general, natural and unexamined sentiments. They were baffled by the infinite mystery, which they saw with a kind of critical ecstasy in the smallest details of life, and were unable to find in the words and forms of their time a medium adequate to convey the new particularity of their conception. And so in trying to use realistically and mystically forms which for three centuries in Italy, France and England had served to carry the voice of nature, artifice or sentiment, they were bound to distort them, breaking up their harmony, and expressing through them as often the false fantastic as the true, and only rarely succeeding in expressing a higher, because more consciously human, realisation of life. Their pursuit of the infinite led them to attempt in language the union of the most distant and sundered details, a good man and a telescope, the breast of a woman and a far country possessed by savages, love and physic,—as if they wished to prove by an arbitrary reconciliation of opposites the absolute unity of life.

A reaction towards an orderly materialism and a humbler propriety was inevitable.

CHAPTER V

THE AUGUSTAN AGE

How have you left the ancient love
That bards of old enjoy'd in you!
The languid strings do scarcely move!
The sound is forc'd, the notes are few.

BLAKE.

Hard is the way and shut the gate,
And life is in a narrow strait.

R. W. DIXON.

I

PURITANISM, then, despite its narrow prejudice, emphasised the reality of the human will. At first, inevitably, its moral egotism seems mean and insignificant after the instinctive amplitude of the preceding age. In every great cycle of art we see an uncritical creative period dwindling into dogma. But in the definition of dogma, however narrow, reason becomes self-conscious and self-respecting; and when the dogma breaks down before a new creative impulse, that impulse is itself more critical and more profoundly rational for the captivity which man has served in the Egypt of hard doctrine and rigid opinions. Thus in the late seventeenth and eighteenth centuries we see a poetry which began in dogma, wit and satire, in an exaggeration of mental conceits,

117

and of which even the licence had ceased to be natural and had frozen into a fashion, gradually returning to reality, as the mind, apprenticed to dogma, grows more actively and habitually critical, pruning first the excesses of its own conceit and mocking at its own artificial licence. Finally, when passion once again awakes to spurn the tyranny of wit, reason is grown powerful and conscious enough to inform the wider experiences which man is ready to embrace as it never did before, to humanise instinct, and upon a basis of natural impulse to rise to a more distinctively ideal conception of the universe.

This in brief is the process visible in English poetry from the time of Dryden to that of Blake, from Cowley to Shelley.

It may be asserted with some truth that wit is outside the province of idealism; for it deals with the secondary realities of life, with the passing manners, and not the eternal morals of a man, with trivialities rather than essentials. Wit criticises life from outside; it plays lightly over its surface, demanding regularity and flatness, and turning any exaggeration it finds to the uses of satire or drollery. It does not wish to discover truth or realise life, but to enforce order from outside. It is not interested in the primary impulses which function beneath the crust of circumstance, and without a knowledge of which life remains either a frivolous pastime or a disorderly spectacle. And since it accepts life materially, it has no yearning to reshape it imaginatively nearer to a considered perfection. Yet the poetry of wit, no less than that of instinct, is intimately related to idealism. The pure idealist combines the critical and creative faculties in absolute proportion. He discovers the nature of things imaginatively, instinct enabling him to identify himself with every form of life, reason to exercise his human power of discrimination. In an instinctive age the creative impulse is stronger than the critical intelligence; in an age of wit the critical powers dwarf the creative sympathies; in the one truth is sacrificed to life, in the other life to logic. Yet through the exercise of wit man slowly mounts from logic to reason, while creative excess degenerates from a sense of universal forces to the licence of private appetite.

The predominant weakness of Augustan poetry is its lack of either sympathy or imagination. The mind is neutral when not prejudiced; it is never inspired, but judges detail on its face value, and therefore submits life, often unfairly, to its ridicule, because it cannot appreciate motive, but only manner. It is strong-minded because narrow-minded; for, seeing but a short distance, it can rule so limited and superficial a consciousness with striking efficiency, and be incisive, vigorous and orderly even in its prejudice.

Such minds are not interested in humanity so much

K

as in types, in public characters, social or political, rather than in simple men expressing an individual humanity. For where the basis of an art is only mental cunning, its subject is bound to be the artificial conditions of its time and the accidents of place and person. It lacks that catholic impulse which compels a man not only to feel universally but to synthesise his inductions. Without this broad basis in nature a poet will confine himself to clever criticism of incidents and disclaim the need of a vital philosophy.

The Augustan was above all a period of satire, and of satire too, which, though often brilliant and entertaining, was also at times cruel with the mean spite of political partisanship. All satire, though at its best inverted sympathy, must transgress to a certain degree that sensibility which is one of the basic principles of poetry, although it may conform to its other principle, which is candour.

For the pure poet does not debase himself to the level of worldly values. He neither desires to trounce a political opponent nor to versify, however brilliantly, a club-room's scandal, but, impelled by the passion for truth rather than for verbal victory, he seeks to divine and so recreate the subtleties of human character, even in its most vicious expression. Thus, however depraved a nature he may discover, he contents himself with rendering its truth, with compassion, too, rather than insult. The whole end, however, of much Augustan satire, was to attack literary or political opponents with every form of exaggerated and petty slander. The justice of such attacks was never considered. The only virtue was to succeed in an unscrupulous battle of wit. In the light then of ideal poetry, how distorted and pompously petty is even such a satire as Dryden's *Absalom and Achitophel*, though satirically how sublime! Even Pope, whose satire was never so savage, because never so creatively strong as Dryden's, admitted in Dryden the prostitution of genius to ignoble ends:

> Ill-fated Dryden! who unmoved can see
> Th' extremes of wit and meanness join'd in thee!
> Flames that could mount and gain the kindred skies,
> Low-creeping in the putrid sink of vice.

The nature of satire is to be ruthless, to satisfy wit at the expense of heart, and it is difficult to satisfy the one without outraging the other. It is curious also, and illuminating, as proof of the frequent barrenness of mere scholarship, to note that the poets of this century, who prided themselves on the accomplished graces of classical learning, who were humanists of the school of Horace, were thus the most signal sinners against humanity itself!

2

Paganism, as we have already noted, degenerates perforce into satire. Its instinctive vitality fails with time, until at last we find the mind unspiritualised, indulging a dry and caustic humour at life's expense. The Elizabethan age was primarily Pagan, and the poets who follow it pass through decadence into satire. Donne combines animalism and cynicism most completely, and because he was honest in both, not only his passion, but also his satire is sincere and serious. It is not cruelly flippant or unpleasantly extravagant as that of many of his contemporaries. But the other element in Donne, his frustrated hunger for eternity, we have seen happily satisfied in the mystical poets; and we have urged that, unlike Donne, they experienced the eternal by avoiding the material rather than by reconciling the two. They identified themselves with the life-force, the positive principle of nature, without criticising its expressions, from a human standpoint, or examining how in fact it asserted itself in the animal world. In short they viewed the earth as disembodied spirits, rather than as men, and their creative ecstasy implies an escape and practises a celestial illusion.

Consequently, Paganism, never truly differentiated even in this heroic attempt to reach a plane of perfect and joyous equilibrium, reasserted itself, but of a meaner quality, since it was more calculated. It possessed no longer the spontaneous physical energy by which earlier it had wedded the universal. Men continued to indulge their instincts, but without the justification of youth's primitive naturalism, and the poetry and drama of the late seventeenth and early eighteenth centuries abounds in the conscious filthiness of accomplished and exhausted roués. The children of those who had castigated their flesh under a system of superstitious asceticism, restored the balance of nature by indulging their own with a superfluity of licence. It is, of course, a mistake to attribute immorality to the poets or dramatists themselves, as, for example, Macaulay did in his celebrated essay. Such a dramatist as Wycherley represented dramatically a section of the life of his time, which was degraded by loose morals. It was not for him to amend or conceal it. The attempted adulteries out of which he makes often such good comedy, were incidents typical of the time, which a contemporary dramatist could not neglect, and no one, in fact, could be a truer moralist than Wycherley, when he revealed with a fine disgust a form of vice even lower than the game of lust itself, namely, the pretence of refinement and virtue as a cloak to lewdness. Nevertheless, the Restoration Drama gives a candid picture of the level to which refinement or sincerity of soul had sunk. The strong extravagance of natural genius, as imaginative as it was often brutal, in the Elizabethan dramatists, was here degenerated into the materialism of a weak excess. Attenuated desire had become the vulgarest because the most sophisticated of appetites. Such calculated licence dishonoured literature for but a brief space; for it lacked even

the sincerity of that honest lust, of which Milton
wrote:

> Belial came last, than whom a spirit more lewd
> Fell not from heaven, or more gross to love
> Vice for itself.

But the children of those who, also inspired by the
spirit of Puritanism, had not castigated, but escaped
the flesh, in an ideal and mystical surrender to
the purest elements in nature, degenerated no less
surely, not into licence but into logic.

The enthusiasm of sense, which forced on man
the imaginative standpoint, because all the world
was to him one great and rare sensation, had in the
course of nature failed.   Man is more and more
by the circumstances of social life and of intellectual
growth separated from his origins.   And his mind
in the process of cultivating self-consciousness cannot at first recapture rationally what he has lost
instinctively.   He is left isolated half-way between
a sensation of the universe and an acquired knowledge of it.   His critical perception only rules his
immediate foreground.   He can analyse, but he cannot synthesise.   Where the instinct of the Elizabethans roved across continents, insatiably curious,
the mind of the Augustans, being as yet a limited
if disciplined mechanism, confined itself to details,
which it selected and arranged.   The Augustan
criticised his sensations, and refined upon the manner
of their indulgence, not upon their quality.   He was

elegant in his obscenity and generally cruel in his wit. He discriminated on a basis of cunning and to the end of material pleasure. In poetry he did not create by absorbing life and then reproducing it, heightened or modified by his personality, but regarding it externally as the mind alone must, he adapted its incidents to suit the requirements of a worldly outlook and a contemporary taste, which delighted, above all, in the poor humour of adultery discovered or the invective of political spite.

We are not considering here the relation between idealism and formal beauty, but, even if we question the practical application of Croce's theory that conception and expression in art are one, we may admit that the more searching or comprehensive the idea, the less can it be disentangled from the matter of its expression, and the less does manner count in itself. For the idealist creates out of the appearance of nature or of man, moments of permanent reality; he dominates the material of life with such power that the medium only exists in our minds as an expression of passionate perception. In short, no matter survives unpervaded or unpenetrated by this vital perception; it has passed through the fire of the poet's truth, and everything irrelevant to the truth which he has conceived has been burnt away. Of the form therefore as a thing distinct we are scarcely aware. Only when the idea fails to find matter suitable for its expression, or when it is too weak or trivial to infuse

the matter with organic life, do we become conscious
of errors, or even felicities, of form regarded as form.
In many poets of the late seventeenth and early
eighteenth centuries we are conscious of little else.
Indeed we flee in gratitude or weariness from their
matter, be it offensive or merely insipid, to the minor
graces of clever craftsmanship, to the elegancies
and verbal clichés which abound. Even Rochester,
weakest of libertines, voices the lust of a lackey in
the language of a lord, adorning his sensualism with
a nice appreciation of the delicately alluring, while
Waller and Suckling, who, we suspect, had little more
perception of the pure truth of Love than the most
frivolous or languishing of coquettes, are artists in
their confectionery. The truth is that these poets
dare not devote themselves to life. Even their
sensualism was trivial, and so they could concentrate
their powers on decoration. This decoration was
admirable, not in so far as it expressed perfectly
an idea, but in so far as its parts balanced, its conceits surprised and its ensemble displayed an agreeable correctness. Such art is comparable in life to
any form of etiquette from which the spirit has passed;
it is like an empty compliment snared in a pretty
phrase, or a dainty piece of porcelain. It is a denial
of idealism, both in its poverty of perception, and in
its failure to develop its form from a genuine internal
necessity. In the wits, no less than in the debauchees
or dandies, the same lack of vision, the same emotional

and intellectual aridity is evident. The substance is provincial, and often mean, akin to the conversation of clubmen or of a society dinner-table; the form is stiff, with the scholastic formulas of the balanced period and the antithesis. Not until the next century do we find such poets as Keats and Byron sincere enough to make the artifices of the heroic couplet or of satire serve the generous impulses of passion and imagination.

Indeed, we might be tempted to say that Puritanism and Latinism between them killed the soul of English poetry for a hundred years, were it not that no creeds or traditions can affect art in themselves. The nature of man was arrived at that point where a certain narrow Puritanism and an artificial Classicism best answered to its needs. Against all that was moral in Puritanism this generation at first rebelled. It accepted only all that was mental in it, to which its narrow egotism responded, and turned its new-found wits to the dressing of licence or invective in faded garments, borrowed from a Latin wardrobe. For when Englishmen ceased to feel strongly, they discovered the mind, and that they had not yet evolved any poetic method for expressing a consciously critical content; and they modelled their style therefore on foreign formulas, particularly Latin, which became in their hands a regular mechanism, calculated to give a pompous appearance to insignificant opinions. But just as Johnson by the

force of his character and the sincerity of his prejudices could in prose give to this artificial manner
a human validity, so Dryden and Marvell and Pope
could occasionally escape from the dreary neat mono-
tony of wit into moments of pure imagination. We
are not questioning the value of wit or of erudition
as activities of the human mind. We merely assert
that they function on a level distinct from that of
idealism; that they set themselves boundaries of fact
which they will not pass, and that within these
they exercise their ingenuity to present facts or
opinions with such shrewdness or blandishment
as will entertain their audience quite irrespective
of the truth. Their judgment, if it pretends to logic,
exercises it only on externals, and far from seeking
for the essentials, delights to exaggerate errors artificially, and excludes all vision unattainable by the
calculating intelligence. This is the very antithesis
of idealism, which loves all forms of life with such
self-forgetful passion that it would apprehend the
reality of each one, and through them that of the
universal spirit of nature. In Marvell, in Dryden,
and even in Pope, this coincidence with the elemental
idea occurs every now and then, either because for
a moment they escape from the limits of mental
consciousness into imagination, or because, as most
frequently in Pope, they exercise their powers of
mental observance with such accuracy that in a perfect delineation of the fact they convey also its

essential nature. We may best illustrate this by three examples. First in Marvell's well-known poem, *The Coy Mistress*:

> Had we but world enough and time,
> This coyness, lady, were no crime.
>   . . . I would
> Love you ten years before the Flood,
> And you should, if you please, refuse
> Till the conversion of the Jews;
> My vegetable love should grow
> Vaster than empires and more slow.

This is ingenious fancy;

> But at my back I always hear
> Time's wingéd chariot hurrying near,
> And yonder all before us lie
> Deserts of vast eternity.

Here passion has woken, and with it that sense of infinite time and space beyond all calculation, that capturing in a moment of the continents of history. That is imagination, and the voice is the voice of the idealist striving out to more than a vision of the material universe. But the inspiration quickly fails. The mind reasserts itself with its grim acceptance of the fact of death which divides man from eternity and reduces all his dreams and aspirations to a few clods, an earthy smell, and the dust driven on the wind.

> Then worms shall try
> That long-preserved virginity;
> The grave's a fine, and private place,
> But none, I think, do there embrace.

In the last stanza the fact of death accepted leads directly on to a fierce and primitive assault on life, a demand for earthly pleasure, by one who has accepted a materialistic standpoint.

> Let us roll all our strength and all
> Our sweetness, up into one ball,
> And tear our pleasures with rough strife,
> Thorough the iron gates of life.

In this single poem there are combined the half-mental, half-sensual conceits of the Augustans, the idealism of the mystics, and the physical craving and spiritual disillusionment of Donne.

Again, at the beginning of Dryden's *Religio Laici*, before the deadening dogma of theological argument has settled on his four hundred lines of correctly rhymed couplets, we find the breath of pure and comprehensive imagination:

> Dim as the borrowed beams of moon and stars
> To lonely weary wandering travellers
> Is Reason to the soul: and as on high
> Those rolling fires discover but the sky,
> Not light us here, so Reason's glimmering ray
> Was lent, not to assure our doubtful way,
> But guide us upward to a better day.
> And as those nightly tapers disappear
> When day's bright lord ascends the hemisphere,
> So pale grows Reason at Religion's sight,
> So dies, and so dissolves in supernatural light.

There could be no completer statement of the faith which supports all idealism.

So Pope, in an invocation which begins on the trite couplet

> Go, gentle gales, and bear my sighs away!
> To Delia's ear the tender notes convey,

can mount to a level in which passion, if simulated, is at least simulated so well as to convince.

> For her, the feather'd quires neglect their song;
> For her, the limes their pleasing shades deny;
> For her, the lilies hang their heads and die.
> Ye flowers that droop, forsaken by the spring,
> Ye birds that left by summer cease to sing,
> Ye trees that fade when autumn heats remove,
> Say is not absence death to those that love?

Or

> Let nature change, let heav'n and earth deplore,
> Fair Daphne's dead, and love is now no more!

Or, directly following a line of unusual banality, the familiar

> See! from the brake the whirring pheasant springs
> And mounts exulting on triumphant wings:
> Short is his joy; he feels the fiery wound,
> Flutters in blood, and panting beats the ground.
> Ah! what avails his glossy, varying dyes,
> His purple crest, and scarlet-circled eyes,
> The vivid green his shining plumes unfold,
> His painted wings, and breast that flames with gold?

The quality which gives these passages poetic sincerity, in spite of artificial mannerisms, is their exact agreement with and their fine selection from the facts of nature. The great service rendered by Pope to

his age was to recall men from the cultivation of
individual conceits, the abuse of egotism in both
intellectual and verbal extravagances, to the order
and method, the general harmony demonstrated by
nature, and necessary to all healthy art. In him a
love of order may have been no more than a taste
for mental correctness, and a deprecation anywhere
of excess, but in condemning the personal and the
fantastic, the inanities of simulated mysticism, in
" mowing down luxuriant follies far and wide,"
he was preparing men for a sincere return, not only
to the larger manner of nature, but to a perception
of her as a medium through which the individual
could realise himself more profoundly than within
the petty orbit of his own self-consciousness. Just
as Steele and Addison humanised Puritanism,
until it issued from the coffee-houses as a quiet
middle-class morality, sane and temperate, assailing
with whimsical laughter the follies of fashionable
licence, so Pope redressed the balance between pre-
cocities of individualism and the normality of nature.
Nevertheless, in doing so, these men " methodis'd "
nature at the cost of their humanity. Neither Addison nor Pope were profound; they desired only a
return to decency. But in this humble creed of
moral decency and artistic correctness their generation found at last equilibrium, a firm if lowly basis,
in which the naturalism of Paganism and the individualism of Puritanism combined, both purged

of their extravagances. And out of this union, when the new creative impulse came at the beginning of the next century, the idealism of the Revolution sprang, championing, often confusedly, a natural morality and a moral naturalism. From an absolute standpoint then the " Reason " of the Augustans was no " Reason," and the conflict they declared, and so unhappily maintained, between the head and the heart is a false one. The distinction between logic and reason is as profound as that between science and philosophy. " Reason " is something more than conscious calculation; it is the ally and not the foe of instinct. It is the principle which, working in union with all the faculties, guarantees that intensest form of consciousness which we name Imagination. Thus " Reason " does not preside over the Imagination in the manner of logic, as Sir Joshua Reynolds, true to the external and superficial view of his age, announced in his *Discourses*, but resides in Imagination, as the leaven in the lump. While Imagination does not contradict logic, but transcends it.

But idealism with the later Augustans was limited to a critical observance of the facts of nature. It belonged to these men just because their vision was material: they neither saw too much nor too little, and when they applied this limited focus to subjects in which great and generous feeling, with its heightened sympathy, should play a part, the result was such bathos as Dryden's translations from Chaucer and Boccaccio, and Pope's *Eloisa to Abelard*.

That loyal and immolated soul, whom Mr. George Moore has recently recreated for us, in whose letters we hear the intense voice of suffering womanhood, becomes in Pope's poem a languid damsel sighing on a sofa, trembling and tearful, and with a tumult in her vestal veins! When wit tries to interpret imagination, the result is disastrous. These Augustan poets lacked consistently both passion and philosophy: they were rich in manufactured feeling and in sententious platitude, and in a capacity for weaving these into a correct pattern. But conceits ingeniously multiplied do not persuade us of the existence of true sentiment, any more than the personification of all the virtues, vices or moralities in capital letters, convinces us of thought. They are like the Albert Memorial, in which not all the Arts, Sciences, Philosophies, Christian and moral virtues, gesturing together in shining bronze, can persuade us of the necessity of beauty, of wisdom, or of goodness. Their empty impersonality touches our humanity at no point. The "nameless somethings" of abstract terms are significant again of a lack of penetrative intelligence. Allegory is the sign of reflective comment, symbol of creative life. The men who indulged in them to excess looked on art, life, thought and nature from outside: they lacked the secret which admits man behind the veil, and

thus were driven to personify abstractions in their
ignorance of humanity. So Pope:

> Here one poor word a hundred clenches makes,
> And ductile dulness new meanders takes;
> There motley Images her fancy strike,
> Figures ill-pair'd and Similes unlike.
> She sees a Mob of Metaphors advance,
> Pleas'd with the madness of the mazy dance;
> How Tragedy and Comedy embrace;
> How Farce and Epic get a jumbled race.

So Marvell:

> My Love is of a birth so rare
> As 'tis for object strange and high;
> It was begotten by Despair
> Upon Impossibility.

These poets could not escape the abstract, because
they were divorced both rationally and sensationally
from the life-principle, which embodies the universal
idea in the particular fact. They observed only the
particular and the material, and this they could not
universalise save artificially in general terms. The
triumph of wit, which entails the nullification of
feeling, is poetically utter defeat. " To steer between
the extremes," which was Pope's amiable maxim,
is and indeed proved to his generation an excellent
life policy; it is poetical suicide.

As Prior wrote:

> Without Love, Hatred, Joy, or Fear,
> They led—a kind of—as it were:
> Nor Wish'd, nor Car'd, nor Laugh'd, nor Cry'd:
> And so they liv'd; and so they dy'd.

L

Their dread of the abuses of feeling was no doubt justified by the writings of many of their immediate predecessors. But a quality or a truth is not discredited because men have degraded them. If the seventeenth century poets made passion an excuse for artificial caprice, the Augustans allowed their fear of it to deprive their writings of human significance and of that insight, that flashing penetration which pricks out the real from the nebulous.

The dexterity with which the Augustan poets concealed their lack of either comprehensive feeling or thought is astonishing, but it does not save them from inanity. Just as they applied standard labels to emotions, instead of realising them afresh in their own life and poetry, so in thought they allowed sententious platitudes long drawn out in endless repetition to take the place of disinterested understanding.

> The proper study of mankind is man,

although it signifies the reaction of this generation from the diffuse generality to the fact, is a phrase of which most of the virtue lies in the trick of expression, and but a fraction in the sense. And it is typical of all their superficial sophistry. They could juggle with facts, but they could not interpret their reality without which facts are lifeless counters. Far truer is Pope's claim:

> My humble Muse, in unambitious strains,
> Paints the green forests and the flow'ry plains.

It is true of Pope himself, of Thomson, and in a different way of Gray, Collins and Cowper. Where Pope succeeded with nature was, as we have said, in an exactness of observation; and a corresponding exactness of delineation; whether it is of

> Swift trouts, diversify'd with crimson stains,

or of a landscape, or a reflection, or a wind ruffling the woods, he describes the phenomenon with an exquisite precision. Thus, as already noted, he conveys at his best the idea through a perfect record of the fact. And he prepared in this way a line of escape for succeeding poets from the well-bred generalities, or ill-bred elegancies, of an artificial society and a scholastic intelligence. With Thomson there is more sympathy with nature and less analytical observance. He is still, in his *Castle of Indolence*, hampered by classical conventions, but in *The Seasons* a new spring of humanity appears and dissolves in its limpid current the parchment of an arid humanism. He is as little in sympathy with the unruly passions of primitive times as with the barren logic-chopping, or the indolent sensualism of his predecessors. He dreams rather of an age of ideal innocence.

> But now those white unblemished minutes, whence
> The fabling poets took their golden age,
> Are found no more amid these iron times,
> These dregs of life! Now the distempered mind
> Has lost that concord of harmonious powers,
> Which forms the soul of happiness; and all
> Is off the poise within.

That dream of an unreal golden age, preached falsely as a fact by Rousseau, was to awake in men a great new impulse towards idealism, an idealism which was perhaps bound by that element of falsehood in its foundation (the belief that nature was a paradise, rather than " nasty, brutish and mean ") to degenerate into the sentimentalism of the mid-Victorian age, after its first blaze of protest. But to Thomson, perhaps more than any other, the later Romantic poets owed a particular debt. It is equally evident in points of style and in the general humanitarianism and self-absorbed egotism, which they inherited from him and intensified. In such a trivial passage as the following we see that fanciful sentimentalising of nature or man in general, in contradiction of all facts, which was to prove the peculiar weakness of the Romantic temperament, and finally to cause a grim disillusionment. Here it is only laughable. Thomson is describing the effect of a rainbow on a rustic:

> He wondering, views the bright enchantment bend
> Delightful, o'er the radiant fields and runs
> To catch the falling glory; but, amazed,
> Beholds the amusive arch before him fly.

Such picturesque romancing was not to be corrected until Crabbe refused

> real ills to hide
> In tinsel trappings of poetic pride.

But more exact echoes of Thomson we find in

Shelley's *Alastor* as well as in Keats' indolent sensationalism and the visionary enthusiasm which culminated in *Hyperion*; not only too in Wordsworth's feeling for and observance of nature (vastly more intimate and profound than Thomson's though it be), but also in his moralising, and even in details of phrase. Lastly, the two following passages, chosen from *The Seasons*, portend both the philosophic and supernatural curiosity typical of the Romantics and their bold sense of the elemental.

> Nor is the stream
> Of purest crystal, nor the lucid air,
> Though one transparent vacancy it seems,
> Void of their unseen people. These, concealed
> By the kind art of forming heaven, escape
> The grosser eye of man: for if the worlds
> In worlds enclosed should on his senses burst,
> From cates ambrosial, and the nectared bowl,
> He would abhorrent turn; and in dead night,
> When silence sleeps o'er all, be stunned with noise.

And

> Or where the Northern Ocean, in vast whirls,
> Boils round the naked melancholy isles
> Of farthest Thule, and the Atlantic surge
> Pours in among the stormy Hebrides;
> Who can recount what transmigrations there
> Are annual made, what nations come and go?
> And how the living clouds on clouds arise,
> Infinite wings, till all the plume-dark air,
> And rude resounding shore are one wild cry?

Meanwhile in Gray and in Collins we see the tide of new emotion slowly advancing. They are not without their abstractions and their pedantries, but

more and more these are absorbed in the living
necessity of feeling, and that a feeling for man or
nature in their universal aspect, in which scholarship is increasingly forgotten save as an instrument
aiding, not dictating expression. Gray's *Elegy* and
Collins' *Ode to Evening* possess a new note, a new
colouring unattainable in the townish daylight of
Dryden and Pope; they are the proof of a returned
sensibility, in which personality and nature combine.
Man has become a sympathetic, romantic, and a
somewhat melancholy spectator of nature, and so
delights in her twilight for its suggestive lack of
definition rather than for daylight and its fact.

> Now air is hush'd, save where the weak-eyed bat
> With short shrill shriek flits by on leathern wing,
> Or where the beetle winds
> His small but sullen horn.
>
> .   .   .   .   .   .
>
> Then let me rove some wild and heathy scene;
> Or find some ruin midst its dreary dales,
> Whose walls more awful nod
> By thy religious gleams.

The quality of this is not borrowed from Horace,
nor a London coffee-house, nor my lady's boudoir;
it is borrowed by man, with instinct now refined
and subtilised, direct from universal nature. And
however much we may decry the age of wit and
indulgence, of platitude and correctness, we may
admit its evolutionary necessity, and that in teaching
men discipline it prepared them for a new adventure.

3

The assumption, however, that the men of the Augustan age had no feelings, because convention did not permit a display of them, is far from correct. The spirit of an age—particularly if it be a period of unadventurous reaction from excess — can dictate not only men's conception of life, but also the very form through which they express it. But it cannot transform human nature. The cult of " correctness," of so-called " reason," which the Augustans adopted had inevitable consequences. Johnson's gloomy tenderness, Swift's malignity, Shenstone's hypochondria, Gray's melancholy, Smart's and Cowper's madness attest a secret warfare. These men suffered acutely for the arbitrary check imposed upon their generous impulses. They rebelled against the harmony of life, against that truth of which Cowper sang:

> 'Tis woven in the world's great plan,
>   And fixed by Heaven's decree,
> That all the true delights of man
>   Should spring from Sympathy.

And life, mocking their logic, tortured them with pain and sickness. It filled them with a baffled desiderium. Only thus could they be liberated. Disillusionment sapped the barriers of intellect. Like blind valetudinarians, groping towards sun and air, they turned from the coffee-house to the country, from the Latin manner to the Greek spirit, from correctness to simplicity and romance, above all to nature, and the gentle moralising which nature provoked.

The return to health was slow and gradual. For long, though conscious of the inadequacy of " reason," they dare not give themselves to life and so refresh their spirits. The first stage was the transformation of the cynic into the sentimentalist. It was only the turning of the same coin, but it was towards the coming light. Man's complacent sense of his own importance gave place to a melancholy sense of his insignificance, relieved by such rare moments of ecstasy as Smart's *Song of David*.

In such poets as Parnell, Shenstone, Akenside and the Wartons, we see emotion too sickly and diffident as yet to capture joy or scan the truth of things — but rather lamenting the cruelty of life and accusing the world and its manners. They had learnt that a cool indifference was a poor substitute for disinterested passion, but not yet that love was the first principle rather than the foe of reason. In Gray and Collins it is the anatomy of scholarship which feeling struggles still too consciously to conquer and transcend, and that reunion of humanity with humanism, comparable to the union of the vernacular with the academic in the Elizabethan age, was quickened both by the ballad revival and by the romantic forgeries of Chatterton and Macpherson. For through the distant and unreal, men escape the conventional and learn to accept the strange, so preparing themselves for the real, which is always both strange and familiar. Apart from their intrinsic literary worth, the impulse set in motion by *Ossian* and the Rowley poems was as considerable as that originated by Allan Ramsay and Bishop Percy, which flowered anew in Robert Burns. Johnson, with grieved determination, and Goldsmith, half-heartedly, might attempt to restore the Augustan dynasty and stem the new emotional tide. But it was running too strongly. The need to relate the ego to some larger harmony, to escape from a conscious mentality, was too pressing. Only so was the serenity men craved to be found. Yet even to so late a poet as the realist Crabbe, the head and the heart seemed inevitable foes, and madness a dread contingency. But in Cowper the mystic release from the material tyranny of time and space is often manifest. " I am neither young nor superannuated, yet I am a child," he wrote. The renewal of a child-like consciousness, the rejection of a worldly, was the aim and to some extent the achievement of Romanticism. By the end of the eighteenth century, criticism and creation were again united on a higher plane, although their union was to prove ideal for but a short period.

4

An age is served by art according to its deserts. And the distinctive qualities of Augustan poetry are artificial content and formal cunning. It presents on the whole a clever but a mean picture of human nature. Yet its pettiness was no doubt inevitable, and if it lack the animal generosity of its predecessor and the spiritual generosity of its immediate successor, it served as the bridge between the two. In evolving and mastering a manner, man escaped the tyranny of matter. He became conscious of his intelligence. And if he withdrew from life for a season and cultivated his fancy and his wit, he returned to it with reason prepared to interpret Nature rather than succumb to her. At first his interpretation may have been imperfect; it was enough that he admitted the need of interpretation and practised it.

It has been the fashion for critics weary of Victorian virtues to condone eighteenth century vices, and exaggerate its contribution to the art of literature and of life. In neither did it appear to advantage. The ages of man and of literary man are identical. A lusty infancy, a boyhood predominantly animal, an adolescence in which the mind gradually asserts itself over the instinct, and then possesses the creature to the temporary exclusion of feeling and the timid and aggressive denial of sentimentalism,—these are the first stages. This adolescent period of epigram and cynicism, based on a small experience of life, replaces that of childish animal spontaneity. It is apt to be exaggerated because the mind is tardy in its growth and fights at a disadvantage against the more quickly developed forces of nature, and so constantly denies nature in fear of being overwhelmed by her. But the mind grows in the very exercise of its cunning, and the creature, confident of his reasoning powers, eventually returns to life and accepts once again vital experiences, which he can now differentiate and turn to noble uses. He has won at last to his first conscious manhood, and he embraces an enthusiastic idealism. He consumes the matter of earth in his own inspired fire, the fire of reason and instinct harmonising in imagination. Later, as the fire of life, so to say, begins to sink, this harmony loses its active equilibrium. His passionate apprehension of spiritual values degenerates either into the repetition of moral platitudes, significant of reason no longer enriched by instinct, or into the languid acceptance of emotion, significant of instinct undiscriminated by reason. Passionate animalism; critical animalism served by self-conscious wit, or in our own day by scientific realism; passionate spirituality, degenerating into romantic sentimentality,—these are the stages of man and of poetry, as history shows us them. The pure animal in his dignity, his universality and his brutality, died, we may say, in our literature with the Elizabethans; the cult of poetical wit passed with the Augustans, of confused idealism with the Romantics, and of sentimentality with the Victorians. It may be that we stand now on the threshold of an age of pure idealism. But the poets of the eighteenth century are of importance because from Donne to Pope, through much sense dissection, wit, licence and arrogance, they developed the mental resources of man. They returned to nature's principles, though blind to her reality, and thus they prepared for the time when poets might go back to life with a new comprehension of their own distinct place and function in the scheme of things. The return was by way of the countryside, and the way of pain and the way of love. If Gray and Collins only for moments escaped completely from the study, Cowper, who had suffered all agonies which brutality can force on too fine a sensibility, sought like a stricken creature fearful of renewed pain the impenetrable comfort of the inanimate world with its peaceful vegetation.

> God made the country, and man made the town,

he cried, and

> Oh for a lodge in some vast wilderness,
> Some boundless contiguity of shade,
> Where rumour of oppression and deceit,
> Of unsuccessful or successful war
> Might never reach me more! My ear is pained
> My soul is sick with every day's report
> Of wrong and outrage with which earth is filled.

That was the spirit of *The Task*, the spirit of return to some calm reality from the noise of men's warring littleness, their conceits and copious chatter and antipathies. Yet Cowper with his disgust of men, with his Calvinistic belief in their incurably original sin, failed to realise the contradiction implied in imputing deep-seated corruption to human nature, and blameless innocence to that inanimate nature of which man is only the most conscious offspring. Nature is innocent only in the sense that she is unconscious of sin; it is a proof of man's superiority in mind that he is aware of it. Doubtless Cowper was too weak and too hurt to take a " bow of burning gold " and " arrows of desire " and confound the life he hated with words of passionate human conviction, or restore to his generation's dwarfed manhood a sense of their lost divinity. He feared a religious hell too much to invite men to heaven. There was indeed in him something of the " coddled poet " which Byron detected. And yet that domestic happiness which he invoked as

> Thou only bliss
> Of Paradise that has survived the fall

lay in the direct line to idealism. For it was based on the bedrock of humanity itself, on the family of man, possibly a little stuffy in Cowper's comprehension of it, a little dominated by sofas, and that " bubbling and loud-hissing urn " which " throws up a steaming column," but for all that true to the organic principle of life, where the poetry that emanated from the club or the boudoir or the theatre stall was only a brilliant or sickly effervescence from the stews of city life.

And in the North there moved and sang a more elemental spirit, nursed on the breast of nature, in revolt against his conditions, depressed by poverty, apprenticed to pain, and yet withal drenched with the very dews of man's simple, struggling, aspiring life, a spirit in whom pathos and defiance alternated, passion and tenderness, hope and despair,—the spirit of Burns. His voice is not the purest nor is its range the widest, but it touches the heart of all men striving after the immortal in the transient, of all men young enough to surrender body and soul to life, and passionate enough to feel the magnetism, the anguish and the insufficiency of flesh, human enough to taste the bitterness of disappointment, and godlike enough to exercise the genius of compassion. Burns touches the hearts of all true and simple men as no poet before him had done, unless it were the unknown minstrels of the ballads. His personal emotion is universal because it is true to all the essentials of human experience, and so kindred in its expression and impulse to nature herself, while distinct in its moral definition.

> O my luve's like a red, red rose
> That's newly sprung in June:
> O my luve's like the melodie
> That's sweetly played in tune.

> As fair art thou, my bonnie lass,
> So deep in luve am I:
> And I will luve thee still, my dear,
> Till a' the seas gang dry.
>
> Till a' the seas gang dry, my dear,
> And the rocks melt wi' the sun;
> I will luve thee still, my dear,
> While the sands of life shall run.

If we compare this with Marvell's *Coy Mistress*, with its conscious playing with the fancy of vast ranges of time, its momentary apprehension of eternity, and its relapse into lusty materialism, we shall measure the change that was come upon poetry.

Here the beauties of nature and of art, the rose and the melody, are utilised to enlarge the human aspect of beauty, they grow naturally out of a human mind conscious of a woman's beauty, and stored with the memories of all the past experiences of beauty in life of which she is the crowning moment; and the passion suggests its eternity, not by escaping into some transcendental region, but by limiting its survival to that of earth herself. Burns expressed the eternal through the momentary, because in his love, while remaining distinctively personal, he was also one with the whole universe in its positive assertion of life, and he proved it by embodying his own emotion in the fairest images drawn from nature and man. In his poetry, as distinct from his life, the creative instinct, with its demand for positive forces in harmony, subdues any destructive elements lurking in the physical impulse out of which the idea sprung. In life maybe, as Keats expresses it, " he talked with Bitches—he drank with blackguards, he was miserable." But the love of his poetry never confines itself to personal desire; in the object of his passion he sees all loveliness, and in all the beauty of the world he sees her reflected and renewed:

> I see her in the dewy flowers,
> I see her sweet and fair:
> I hear her in the tuneful birds,
> I hear her charm the air:
> There's not a bonnie flower that springs
> By fountain, shaw or green,
> There's not a bonnie bird that sings
> But minds me o' my Jean.

This is no mere poetry of the senses, no idle indulgence of them in ornate epithets and delicate similes, nor is his a transcendental experience divorced from life. In Burns rather we see the creature passing through a perception of a fellow creature and of the earth to which he belongs into the mind of the creator. Burns humanises the love of man for woman, and in the combination of the human and the natural he reaches the divine. The fever of earth doubtless in him often destroyed the serenity of heaven. He was a seaman tossed on the universal deep, who only at times put safely into port, to be driven out again on the next high tide.

> Wi' lightsome heart I pu'd a rose,
> Frae off its thorny tree;
> And my fause luver staw the rose,
> But left the thorn wi' me.

The important thing was that men could once again be pricked with thorns or wrecked at sea. Their sensibility had returned, and with it their yearning after wide prospects and impossible perfections, their consciousness of the mud into which they too often fell, and of the serene heavens above their heads.

> But oh! I backward cast my e'e
> On prospects drear!
> An' forward, tho' I canna see,
> I guess an' fear!

M

CHAPTER VI

WILLIAM BLAKE

'Tis Reason, but beyond your ken
There lives a light that none can view
Whose thoughts are brutish:—seen by few,
The few have therefore light divine;
Their visions are God's legions!

GEORGE MEREDITH.

I

OF all idealists William Blake is perhaps the earliest
and the most absolute to be found in English literature, so absolute indeed that to many he has seemed
inhuman or insane. Born late in the eighteenth
century, a humble and unfrequented man, he
escaped the narrowing influences of his time, and
viewing the world of art from no standpoint but that
of impartial sincerity, he became convinced that the
age of mere cleverness and pedantry was to pass
away for ever. He named it the Kingdom of the
Tree of Knowledge, and asserted that those who
tasted its fruit became militant towards each other,
and in their mental self-assurance, set up a barrier
of logic between themselves and the truth of life.

They starved their sensibility until it became dead,
and ceased to enrich their minds with experience.
Thus intellect, negative and mechanical in itself,

stunted their natures, blinded their vision, and withered their sympathies. Not only so, but they became cruel and unforgiving, because they were divorced from that universal life, in which the ego finds its true perspective and ceases to exaggerate its claims or denounce the actions of others as unforgivable sins, but realises that most evil in the world is traceable to ill-adjusted circumstances, for which he who condemns, or the system which he tolerates, may well be responsible. All evil in Blake's opinion can be forgiven, if not actually removed, by understanding. But by understanding he implied a blend of sympathy and reason. It was neither mere sentiment nor mere logic which he termed " a confident insolence, sprouting from systematic reason." The kingdom of the future was, in contrast with the Kingdom of the Tree of Knowledge, that of the Tree of Life, which gave to a man who ate of it a perpetual fellowship with the universe of man and of nature, with life's essential spirit, however it manifested itself. And through his identity with everything, through this wedding with the elements, a man could not condemn anything without condemning himself. He would rather pity error as one who shared at however great remove in its causes and its consequences.

> Can I see another's woe
> And not be in sorrow too?
> Can I see another's grief
> And not seek for kind relief?

And

> To Mercy, Pity, Peace and Love
> All pray in their distress,
> And to these virtues of delight
> Return their thankfulness.
>
> For Mercy, Pity, Peace and Love
> Is God our Father dear;
> And Mercy, Pity, Peace and Love
> Is man, His child and care.

And

> Mutual forgiveness of each vice,
> Such are the Gates of Paradise.

Thus self-love was universalised, and when a man sympathised with everything, he saw things not externally in those transient and material shapes, which the brute intelligence alone can apprehend, but in their essential significance. For he himself shared their idea of life, and in their forms he looked only for that pure idea manifesting itself in ever diverse matter. And being an artist Blake welcomed every phenomenon in which he saw the idea subduing the matter completely to its own expressive desire, so that no idle, irrelevant elements remained, but each particular contributed to the significance of the whole. Thus he writes: " Everything that lives is holy," but the emphasis lies in the word " lives." The purer life is, the more intensely it lives, the more completely it irradiates each element of which it is composed. This is the pure doctrine of idealism, and it embraces the whole of Blake's conception of life. Life was to him primarily a spiritual consciousness, and only secondarily the substance of a creed. The consciousness expresses itself in the simple elation of his lyrics, as subliminal in tone and substance as ever poetry has been. But in his Prophetical Books, letters, notes and Apophthegms, he explained his consciousness to himself as a creed. He subjected this creed to exact analysis, and he found that those who were not idealists, trusting implicitly to a passionate imagination, became the slaves either of their senses or their mind. The former surrendered themselves to nature, who is soft and formless and desires only material increase and sensual excess. This is vegetable nature, as distinct from the creative force working in nature, and he called her in his prophetic books " Vala," a feminine goddess, heavy and indolent, lacking definition or certainty, and fascinating only by a certain luxurious sloth. And he held that those who worship her, show in their art a too passive love of accumulated detail and alluring colours. Such have lost their masculine capacity for discretion and rejection, for a continual refusal to appetite of sensations pleasant in themselves, but subversive to the idea which they are seeking to embody. Like Titian in his more laboured moments, they indulge in the flesh for its own sake, and by continual indulgence their imaginations become clouded, sluggish, and at last impotent, and they accept the matter of life as sufficient in itself.

The struggle, therefore, evident in the natural

world between creative energy and vegetable matter, Blake found to correspond in the world of man to the antagonistic forces of good and evil, in which evil is either an indecisive strife between matter and the idea, resulting in discord, or the triumph of matter over the idea, resulting in the sleep of sensuous death.

Better therefore than this passive acceptance of nature is, in Blake's view, even an excess of passion which destroys the flesh in its revolt from material acquiescence and its pursuit of some prejudiced and personal idea. For the materialist in his art can only imitate nature or repeat her images in uncritical profusion. He can never originate, because he possesses no idea from which to start, and true form can only originate from within. And so he is forced into mere representation of what he does not understand, and into the repetition of sensations which he remembers. This weak surrender to material memory, in place of ever assertive originality, Blake particularly denounces, as being the condition of those who accept the limitations of nature and of fact, and set up habit in place of thought, and allow mannerism to encroach more and more upon sincerity; failing to

> seize the inmost form
> With ardour fierce and hands of flame.

We see the same conflict between memory and active experience occurring in the poetry and philosophy of Keats, symbolised in the persons of Mnemosyne and Moneta. But against the tyranny of mechanical mind Blake spoke no less bitterly. It is logic which he attacks, not reason. For logic represents a mechanical exercise of mind, and is divorced alike from physical sensibility and spiritual vitality. The brain of man is a limited organism which by itself can deal only in material values: it can comprehend fact alone, and it bases its calculations and its judgment on pure externals. It has the precision of law, but its logic, like that of law, is confined within the rules of an artificial text-book, —an exclusive curriculum, manufactured from precedent, and representing in its propriety an imperfect and temporary compromise between primitive error and absolute justice. Such logic to Blake was a barrier against life instead of a true interpretation of it. He would not admit even its temporary necessity: for he considered that it frustrated the good impulses of life far more than it restrained the evil. All dogma to him was a system of thought unconnected with realities, and the conclusions of such thought, however well argued and precise, were false, because based on the transitory material accumulated by memory on facts and deeds and appearances, and not on the ideas, impulses or emotions that went to produce them. Reason was to Blake an activity of mind very different in quality. It was a condition of vital consciousness, a form of thought to which

instinct contributed, and comparable to Bergson's
" intuition." It was a thinking with body and mind
together. For in such an act of comprehension, a
man is possessed by a passionate desire for life, and
thus for identifying himself with the object of his
observance so completely that he learns its inner
nature, reading every material form, freed of all
confusing detail, as a perfect particular symbol
of a true and essential idea. It was to this experience Blake referred when he wrote: " Excuse my
enthusiasm, or rather madness, for I am really
drunk with intellectual vision," or when he said:
" Men are admitted into heaven not because they
have curbed and governed their passions, but because
they have cultivated their understandings," or " the
roadway of excess leads to the palace of wisdom."
And by this he did not mean the kind of cultivation
which Pope practised, a rejection of life in general
and the cultivation of an enclosed patch of it. He
meant that the more passionately a man embraced
the experience of life (and he could not do so too
passionately or too universally) the more must he
develop his reason and train his senses to discriminate
what was transient and accidental from what was
eternal and sprung from creative necessity.

Reason, therefore, he conceived to be a form of
positive activity seeking truth everywhere without
prejudice, and inspired by an infinite yearning, by
that love which comes of a sense of sonship and

brotherhood with all creation. This is that love which speaks in all his lyrics, a love which is not the antithesis of self-love, but the enlarging of it by sympathy into a universal emotion, a love which is ever joyous because it is in the main current of life, and because all pure life is joy. It is the smile of love of which he says:

> And betwixt the cradle and grave
> It only once smiled can be;
> And when it once is smiled
> There's an end to all misery.

But Blake was too true an idealist to be a vague visionary. Indeed, the accusations of incomprehensibility and even insanity which have been so often made against him arose from the fact that he attempted to convey his comprehension of an idea, in words at least, too realistically, too nakedly for men familiar with appearances, rather than essences, to recognise. His ideas were precise enough and constant enough, and they were drawn out of matter rightly regarded, but they partook too little of common humanity in their presentation. He rarely, if ever, showed any of the " mystic's hazy treatment," as critics have so often pleaded in their inability to understand him; but where as a poet he failed was in an accuracy which was almost too mathematical, a vision too anatomic, for human understanding. He often could not restore to the idea, which he had attained by inspired penetration, the flesh of common life. It is true that the idea represented generally some first principle, some elemental life-force for which a human embodiment could not well be discovered, and for these " eternal existences," the features of men and women, with their indecisive graces or mean distortion, could scarcely be used without degrading the divine beings, which his imagination comprehended. But his idealism was sincere and courageous, because he both sought consistently for absolute truth in the matter of life, and ever demanded its embodiment, not in a general vagueness, a transcendental mist, but in a particular definition. Few men with a passion for the " eternities " have avoided so scrupulously the temptation to rhetoric, or striven so zealously to find an exact symbol for a universal concept. " Los " and " Urizen " may be supernatural symbols, but, like " the Ancient of Days," they are drawn with perfect precision. Blake loved the concrete so ardently that he would " circumcise away the indefinite," and he reversed the usual order of opinion and said: " Truth has bounds, Error has none." For truth, he held, is only completely visible where an idea achieves bold and confident form, of which each part is in harmony, and all contribute actively to the desired expression; error shows itself always in vagueness or in chaos, where there is no harmony between the parts, but both exaggeration and lassitude, the invariable condition of an undefined idea. It is against this

condition of protoplasm or irrelevance in art that
he pleaded, when he wrote:

> As poetry admits not a letter that is insignificant, so painting
> admits not a grain of sand or a blade of grass insignificant,
> much less an insignificant blot or blur.

As the creative process is to embody the universal
in the particular, so it is the poet's first business to
see it,—to see as Blake wrote in the lines so often
quoted and perhaps so vaguely comprehended:

> The world in a grain of sand,
> And a heaven in a wild flower;
> Hold infinity in the palm of your hand,
> And eternity in an hour.

And where Blake fails, not in his lyrics, but in his
prophetic books, in clearness and intelligibility, it
is because he has striven after too ultimate and
abstruse an idea, and has attained it incompletely,
so that it refuses an organically precise expression
and can only be conveyed by abstract formulæ. But
general knowledge, as Blake knew, was remote
knowledge: it was not completely mastered by the
consciousness; it was insufficiently realised.

Blake sought to define the elemental energies of
life, Pope the prospect and the conversation of an
urban drawing-room; not unnaturally the one failed
frequently: perhaps the limitation of the other is
sufficiently attested by his invariable success. But
materialists have always exaggerated Blake's incomprehensibility. His reason in its passionate

assault on unassailable heights never once collapsed
into frenzy, it never lost that vision of intellectual
beauty which Shelley was to celebrate, that sense
of spiritual values which the discord of fanaticism
denies. He was ever temperate, but temperate in
the ruling of a divine excess. And his bold and
denunciatory revolt against both art and life when
they are based upon either a languid self-indulgence
of the senses, or on that barren " most murderous
of logics," limited by space and arguing from
memory, was the title to a completely new chapter
in English poetry. And the title ran thus:

> Children of the future age,
> Reading this indignant page,
> Know that in a former time
> Love, sweet love, was thought a crime.

Few of those who trod unconsciously in his footsteps saw their way or the ultimate goal as clearly as
he, and the two who might have reached it death
cut off too soon. But the emancipation from corporeal reason and corporeal sense, which Blake
preached, was to be realised, if imperfectly, in the
early years of the nineteenth century, and a Beauty
seized upon by poets which depended neither on
the manners of a class, nor the tastes of an individual,
nor the elegancies of a style, a Beauty upon which
mimetic skill or mental cunning or social experience
never encroached, the Beauty which is to be found
in the universal matter of man and of nature by

those who devour it with the ardent and impartial eyes of imagination.

2

Here then was a man possessed by the spirit of life; his was the purest, gladdest response to elemental energy, which finds expression in our literature. At first Blake voiced it in simple lyrical ecstasy, clear as crystal, but from *Poetical Sketches* to *Songs of Experience* we watch the transparent dawn of innocence accepting the mingled reality of day. Blake's history as poet and artist is that of a man ecstatically conscious of the creative unity of life, driven to define this spiritual mystery in terms of matter, and to separate life's essence into its component elements. These elements, which ideally should form a creative harmony, but which too often, divorced from one another and self-considering, induce discord, sloth and death, he embodies at last in the great Gothic ruin of his Prophetic Books, peopled by such protagonists of spirit, mind or matter, as Los, Urizen, Luvah and Tharmas.

In tracing the relations of these elements, Blake is beyond time. He consorts with eternities; and yet in less absolute moments his individualism and poetical anarchism only differed from that of kindred spirits of his age in being more extreme.

He was not unique in feeling in his day the bliss

of eternity and the shame of a sordid street. To others than he, earth seemed then only a graveyard awaiting the moment of some glorious resurrection. Blake's revolt against dead formalism, his hatred of passivity was more purely artistic, more imaginatively absolute even than Shelley's, and so when his imagination failed of an absolute vision of reality, he fell, not into revolutionary rhetoric or egotistic sentiment, as others did, but into pure nonsense. These moments of visionary chaos, when facts are not completely transmuted into spiritual symbols, but all is blurred, are of no value to anyone. Pre-eminently modern, however, Blake is, as the first consciously to distinguish man's position in the economy of life; and unlike many later Romantics he never for a moment sentimentalised or moralised over Nature. " Nature," he said, " is the work of the devil . . . the devil is in us, as far as we are Nature." But for him this " devil " was potentially divine. He looked forward to the time when divided man should win a higher unity, conscious and creative, in which love and reason and life should be one, and energy an eternal delight. His aim was to refashion the broken harmony of the present by bidding men be more pitying than Puritanism, to cultivate an ever active vision and live positively at peace.

CHAPTER VII

WORDSWORTH

To lie in the name of poetry is an offence for which a man may not be forgiven. Experience must do the work of innocence as soon as conscience begins to take the place of instinct.—SWINBURNE.

I

THE extent of mankind's indebtedness to different poets can never be calculated, but we may claim with confidence that Wordsworth has exercised a profound influence over many to whom poetry otherwise meant very little. No man on his own confession was less sensitive to emotion than John Stuart Mill. His whole education had emphasised analysis at the expense of sympathy, the drill-sergeant had mechanised a shrewd individuality, and had certainly upset that balance among the faculties by which the ardours of life continue to break down the barriers which logic would set up. His tendency was ever to be more a machine than a man. Yet when life took its revenge upon him for a too persistent attitude of criticism, and left him to his calculations, unblessed by any sense of pleasure or necessity, and unsupported by those vital impulses which make a merely intellectual journey a thing of exciting incident, it was Wordsworth's poems which proved a medicine to his mind, and saved him from becoming a chronic prey to colourless depression.

They seemed [he writes] to be the very culture of the feelings, which I was in quest of. In them I seemed to draw from a source of inward joy, of sympathetic and imaginative pleasure, which could be shared in by all human beings; which had no connexion with struggle or imperfection, but would be made richer by every improvement in the physical or social condition of mankind. From them I seemed to learn what would be the perennial sources of happiness, when all the greater evils of life shall have been removed.

Yet of the poet who could inspire such a sense of joy and admiration, he also wrote, " There have certainly been, even in our own age, greater poets than Wordsworth "; and, " Compared with the greatest poets, he may be said to be the poet of unpoetical natures."

Such limited strictures have often been repeated by smaller men who lacked the judgment or the sincerity to recognise the majesty that was Wordsworth's as well as the platitude, and we think it profitable even after so many have already trodden the path, to examine afresh both the qualities of which the greatest poetry truly consists and the extent to which Wordsworth exemplified them. For although the failure of rationalists to appreciate poetry may often be imputed to the limitations of minds trained to logic, to withered sensibilities, and a hearing deaf to music, yet it has been at least partly due to defects in the poetry which such men have first approached, either by mischance or misled by the uncritical voice of popular applause; and to those distortions of truth enshrined in picturesque phraseology which they have been quick to discover, because by nature they respond less readily to any merely sentimental appeal. Such indeed was the misfortune of Mill himself, who found in Byron only a passionate expression of the discontent from which his own mind was temporarily suffering. Yet no poetry, however attractive its imagery or alluring its music, is of the first order which can be proved to transgress reason in the widest application of the term. The greatest poetry is the most beautiful, but also the most profoundly true, and the rationalist deserves our gratitude when he refuses to accept a poem, however magnetic its language or its form, the substance of which he realises to be false. The veritable music of Apollo is only degraded and forgotten if it be confused with the seductive song of the Sirens.

But it is said that poetry is independent of truth, that the poet is concerned only with his personal feeling, that it is enough if the feeling, whatever its quality, be intense, for it will then find impassioned and rhythmic expression and convince others of its reality. It will thus be true to nature in so far as it is vital in its impulse, and to man in so far as it represents a possible human experience. Much

N

lyrical poetry is personal sensationalism of this kind. Yet that alone has achieved any permanency which, if true to the poet's momentary impulse, has also proved true to some deeper and more constant law. For, creatively original as a poet must be, neither his feeling nor his thought are independent of the phenomenal world, or the general consciousness. It may be that he can create imaginatively a more beautiful world than that he sees about him, as Spenser does, or Shakespeare in Prospero's isle, but even this, if it is to be more than a work of pure fantasy, must imply a criticism of actuality, and can invariably be proved to represent an intensification and a reshuffling of the elements of life to produce a higher harmony. If a poet, through being true as he thinks to himself, prove false to nature, he satisfies no personality but his own, and life, which is pitiless to those who slight her, expels him from the circle of human interests. Even lyrical poetry, therefore, which aims at the direct expression of human emotion, must prove true to more than arbitrary impulse if it is to excite human sympathy. It is possible, for example, that a man in a peculiar condition of health, or stimulated by a drug, may experience unusual sensations because his perception of life at the moment is distorted, yet a record of such sensation, however intimate and picturesque, is at best a bizarre or morbid entertainment. It falls short of the truth and dignity of great art. The symptoms of the sick man or the delirium of the fever patient are accidental and partial; they are matter for the pathologist. As Goethe has said, " If the poet is ill, let him first of all cure himself. When he is cured he will write."

Poetry, then, must generally represent a compact between the idea of man and the fact of the natural universe, between the individual mind and the universal matter; and although a poet may recreate that universe nearer to his heart's desire, or, choosing some force or element in it, express this in its pure essence, purged of all such gross matter as prevents its perfect expression in life, he cannot contradict life without courting death for himself. Originality consists not in a blind and arbitrary assertion of the self, but in a revelation through the self of that absolute existence of which man is but a partial interpreter. Man by right of sonship owes duties to the universe which may not lightly be disregarded. To neglect them is to invite certain disinheritance.

The rights of personality have, however, too often been advanced in defence of a contorted egoism, of private emotions intensively cultivated, until they cease to bear any relationship with the positive forces of life, whether physical or spiritual, but caricature reality. For the distinction between heightened spiritual insight and sensational excess or fanciful extravagance lies just in this—that the one interprets the universe, the other distorts or

denies it. A poet may deny the world of actuality
the better to image his own absolute values by the
creation of perfect beauty, or he may accept it and
attempt to reconcile the conflict between its actuality
and his desire in some vision of the future towards
which he believes the world to be tending, or stress
with passionate resignation the gulf that for ever
divides them. But the one thing forbidden to him is
to confuse the two, to gratify his desire by varnishing
the world. A great poet must be true to himself,
but however transcendent his consciousness, in
whatever "worlds unrealised" he may seem himself
to be moving, he must relate that consciousness
to the conditions of the material world about him.
Certainly his sympathy with life must be critical,
if he is to rise above the animal or the sentimental,
but it must be creative too, and it must admit the
part which the universe plays together with the
individual in the creative process.

A misapprehension, however, of what passion in
poetry implies, and the worship of it for its own
sake independently of its content, has led to much
error. Passion is the active expression in man of
the vital force: it is the agent alike of all creation
and all destruction. We have all seen a wind tearing
through the elms in mid-June, or a garden lapsing
into formless luxuriance for the want of restraining
culture, and we know this to be the fruit of life no
less than the rose unfolding itself under a quiet

sky. So it is with poetry; passion is its principle, but excess confounds it: passion rightly directed enables a man to transcend material bounds, and, seeing into the truth of things, to create " forms more real than living man"; unco-ordinated by his reason it may reduce him to a fiend, destroying all that comes into his path. Without passion a man lacks imagination—he can only view and record facts or gratify his senses by garnishing facts with fancies. Passion makes him one with the spirit of life, constant behind all fleeting material forms, and he can therefore resolve these forms at will into their elements and recreate them with more significance. Poets have often employed myths or allegories to convey their imaginative vision of the essential beauty of life, and this, possibly more than anything else, has led the rationalist to distrust their veracity. Yet the poet seeks only to convey truth the more vividly through creating an existence distinct from the normal and the habitual. He has pierced through the crust of life to those principles which work together for beauty and harmony, and so for creative truth; and he exercises a creator's prerogative in embodying these in a new world of his own imaginative construction. The whole purpose of illusion is to present the idea of life which the poet has apprehended, in its purest and most arresting form, by disentangling it altogether from the world of ordinary occurrence which man has grown to accept as final and inevitable. When the illusion is true, the poet, far from indulging his taste for the fantastic, is seeking to express the truth which he has experienced in life, only the more intensely by himself creating a new world for its clearer manifestation. That the structure, therefore, of poetry may seem to contradict nature is no proof of its falsehood. For it may transcend nature. In nature herself life reveals itself in a million different forms, and we ask of the poet only that his idea should be true, and that his form should give to that idea adequate expression. If he imagines a world distracted by warring energies or a character enervated by selfish indulgence, we demand merely that he create these true, both in type and particular, and we must in all justice condemn him if he veils their reality beneath manufactured beauty, and so seeks to excite sensuous pleasure in us at the cost of spiritual honesty. The creative vigour with which he embodies his vision, however terrible it be, will give us a truer pleasure, while only a deep apprehension of life-forces blending one with another in harmony can truly deserve or admit that form of Beauty, the ultimate aim of every artist, which satisfies both the soul yearning after a stainless world, and the mind which has accurately read the imperfections under which the world still labours.

Both Beauty, therefore, and ugliness are truth, and truth, whatever its nature, passionately apprehended

and created anew, is potential Beauty, and the truer
poet is he who, loving all things, is admitted to the
inner knowledge of them, and understanding both
their weakness and strength, their harmony and their
too frequent discord, would fashion a life in which
only creative values exist in absolute agreement:
but who does not shrink from visioning truthfully
all that contradicts his desire in the world that is.

2

No poet sought more zealously than Wordsworth
to avoid the abuse of both personality and passion
to which the conditions of his age so perilously
invited. The effect of the French Revolution and of
the ideas of which it was only the physical manifestation was to encourage a contempt for " reality " and
a hasty exaggeration of personal values. There
hovered in the air above all the squalor and savagery
of brutal passions let loose

> The splendour, which had given a festal air
> To self-importance.

It filled the most sensitive minds of that generation
with a sudden exultation and a fevered excitement.
As Wordsworth said:

> The wings
> Of speculation, joyfully outspread,
> Hovered above our destiny on earth.

It was this combination of powerful self-consciousness and sudden mental and emotional emancipation

which explains the false elements in Romanticism. In the actual world it may often happen that the " throwing off oppression must be work as well of Licence as of Liberty "; but the tragedy is increased when the disease of violence infects the world of ideas, misleading even philosophic minds and blinding sensitive spirits. That it did so in the early years of the nineteenth century cannot be doubted; we see its effects in every line of life. In poetry particularly it led men to deify the human will and to cultivate every passion and sensation irrespectively, whence came a wasteful unrest, and the spectacle of instincts craving in dissatisfaction or satiety for what they knew not. A universal hunger was abroad which urged men to batten upon the elements, and resulted too often in their battening upon neighbour or friend. On the one hand Rousseau's sentimental preaching of natural virtue encouraged men to abandon both intellectual judgment and human responsibility, and to justify excess of whatever kind because it seemed to imply an assertion of individuality. The situation was indeed paradoxical in which men surrendered the whole veto power of the human will in their eagerness to emphasise its rights. On the other hand the casuistry of Godwin came with all the precision of logic to supplement the sentimentalism of Rousseau in a creed of mechanical reason, seeming to sanction the arrogances of egoism by deifying an abstract intelligence, divorced from human experience, and so from human values. But the result in poetry of this logical and sentimental egoism was twofold. Either in the impulse of a passion naturalistic in origin poets rose to heights of pure illumination, and communed, as Shelley did, with the forces of life as with elemental spirits, or, blindly rebelling against fact, whether embodied in a moral or social code or in accepted tradition, they indulged their own passions, gratified selfish emotions and sentimentalised their own lust.

It was this failure to face facts and to balance the claims of man with the laws of life which led to moral and æsthetic anarchy, and to that cult of weak and pitiful melancholy, of Byronism and Werterism, which became the sickly fashion of the times. Poets alternated between a mystical Pantheism, a mechanical Rationalism, and a sensuousness which grew morose as disenchantment stole over their consciousness. In this world of vigorous confusion, swinging rudderless between cosmic inspiration and inhuman selfishness, Wordsworth appears like a rock, lined and riven by the storm, forbidding at times in its scarred solemnity, at others bathed in the mellow sunlight, but always standing secure in its foundations. For his was " The self-sufficing power of solitude,"

> A desolation, a simplicity,
> To which the trappings of a gaudy world
> Make a strange background.

Wordsworth, in short, is the poet of evolution in a time of revolution. We see it even in his style. For in spite of his attack on poetic diction, no Romantic poet shows so clearly the influence of the more liberal writers of the eighteenth century, of Thomson and Akenside, Goldsmith and Dyer, whose *Fleece* he so highly praised. Even the moralising tendencies and didacticism, which trespassed sometimes disastrously on Wordsworth's imagination, were the inheritance of a generation which admired Young's *Night Thoughts*. Abstraction and its inflated phraseology united in Wordsworth with the mysticism of new-awakened passions. Yet the prosaic solemnity, the languid sermonising traits in him, have been much exaggerated. All true art is moral, as is all true science: they should both offer man a sermon in how to live with positive virtue, in passionate communion with beauty and with truth. It is as parochial-minded to separate poetry from true moral life as it is to tie religion to dogma or state-policy, or to encourage science to feed the armouries of the world. Would we live or would we die, in thought, in feeling or in action,—that is after all the question of morality: and the arts, the sciences, the philosophies are on the side of life or are unworthy the name, and must be relegated to the world of parlour pastimes, academic exercises or rigid dogmas. Without morality we know not when we are destroying life and when creating it, when merely accumulating matter and when vitalising it so that it assumes form. We become creatures of habit or of licence, and make the best of things as they are, which is the deadly virtue of fools. For true morality is the index of universal knowledge, the synthesis of a liberal and penetrating experience. It is the " open eye " of Reason, pointing direction to a man " By soul-engrossing instinct driven along," enabling him to create in a divine excess, rather than to destroy in a demoniacal fury or desert the active arena for the sentimental drug-shop. In this sense Wordsworth is moral, as are Shakespeare and Goethe and Meredith, and unlike, generally, Pope, or Byron or Tennyson, who are wise in maxims, cynical, sentimental or luxurious as the moment invites, and who, submitting their art to contemporary standards, amuse and gratify rather than liberate and enlighten. For to be truly moral is to search passionately, above and beyond legal correctness, after ideal truth, and to refuse all forms of beauty and pleasure, all conventions which reflect reality impurely. Byron thought that to break conventions was enough; but he spurned the weeds of falsehood more often than uprooted them, and when he destroyed with justice he had little truth to plant in the desolated soil. Both the character and career of Wordsworth are in studied and refreshing contrast. He of all men by birth and upbringing was incapable both of affectation and of easy charm, and was tempera-

mentally equipped to remind men of the simple
and sincere truths that should govern human relationships; those, so to say, domestic realities which
persist unchanged while the body and mind of
man accept in the school of life the chastisement
of experience, and humanity becomes more and
more competent to direct its destiny, whether
towards evil or good. Wordsworth's own history
is poetically the one greatly sane spectacle to be
found in a period of feverish and tearful revolt
against mental and social cant, of spasmodic sentimentalism and spiritual hypochondria. How much
of his stability he owed to his early environment
in that ideal democracy of hills, we need not enquire.
That composure and dignity of soul, that intense
tranquillity which we associate always with the
truly great man, must certainly have been reinforced
by the example of nature.

> Early had he learned
> To reverence the volume that displays
> The mystery, the life which cannot die:
> But in the mountains did he feel his faith.
>
> There was a hardness in his cheek,
> There was a hardness in his eye,
> As if the man had fixed his face
> In many a solitary place,
> Against the wind and open sky!

For the character of the Lake country stamps itself
on those who live in the shadow of its hills, or fight

their way across its fells in the teeth of wind and rain. Grandeur and simplicity unite there, power and humbleness. The ecstasy and illumination of vast prospects and almost supernatural horizons is balanced by a continual consciousness of the inflexibility of earth, of her strength and constancy in all weathers; softened, but not weakened, by sunshine; as impervious to the raging storm as to the hovering mist; silent amid the tumult of the heavens. The sense of eternity, powerful though it must be to all who tread the heights of Helvellyn or Scawfell, is rivalled by the sense of necessity. Nowhere perhaps in the world does Nature reward man with more moments of absolute revelation, or chasten him with more hours of patient submission to the powers that be. The joy born of such a solitude is only the more profound because it has to conquer an imminent sense of the fatality of natural forces before it can exist. The feelings there are not lightly excited, but when aroused they have the depth, the calm, and the tenacity of earth.

Thus the elemental and moral qualities which are Wordsworth's most striking attributes, the desire for Liberty and the recognition of law, were learnt from life rather than as bookish precepts. From childhood he must have been to Nature as one

> Nursed in his Mother's arms, who sinks to sleep
> Rocked on his Mother's breast, who with his soul
> Drinks in the feelings of his Mother's eye.

Add the circumstance that he was

> Born in a poor district, and which yet
> Retaineth more of ancient homeliness,

and we can believe that early environment contributed much to the heartening consistency of his career, that it was the original source of that power upon which he drew to conquer the distractions and pierce the delusions of his time, and to subdue his own too hasty and rebellious instincts.

For he, too, succeeded to that "bright tradition of the golden age" which was his generation's peculiar and fatal possession. Never was life in itself more valued and less criticised.

> Bliss was it in that dawn to be alive,
> But to be young was very Heaven! O times
> In which the meagre, stale, forbidding ways
> Of custom, law and statute, took at once
> The attraction of a country in Romance!
> When Reason seemed the most to assert her rights
> When most intent on making of herself
> A prime enchantress.

A glorious time, as only enthusiastic youth can be, but dangerous to men unable to distinguish the true enchantress from the false!

Yet to Wordsworth it offered less temptation to spiritual or physical licence than to others. Intuitive beliefs and soaring aspirations were his, optimisms too easily accepted, and still to be tried in the scorching fire of disillusionment; but the faith which shed a supernatural glory about his early manhood was neither metaphysical nor sentimental. It was born of his own generous instinct, and of that enraptured intercourse with nature, which had been his since childhood. It grew out of communion with the universe and with the heart of unsophisticated man; and so, when the dreams of a restored Paradise vanished before the reality of a Napoleon, the conviction survived, though much shaken by doubt, disgust, and despondency, that

> A gracious spirit o'er this earth presides
> And o'er the heart of man.

The belief, of course, in any immediate realisation of this truth in social or national life had of necessity to be abandoned in favour of a theory of gradual evolution, to which both Shelley and Keats turned for an explanation of all those monstrous facts which outraged their sense of beauty.

> Neither vice nor guilt,
> Debasement undergone by body or mind,
> Not all the misery forced upon my sight,
> Misery not lightly passed, but sometimes scanned
> Most feelingly, could overthrow my trust
> In what we may become.

Wordsworth had travelled far and by dark ways from the rapturous period of his youth when he wrote this. By nature proud and intolerant, with strong animal instincts, he had humbled himself to accept practical defeat at the hands of life. He had brought his faith and the world to judgment, and it was the latter which he had found wanting.

It is the inevitable experience of the poet who would be both the prophet of to-morrow and the practical evangelist of to-day. And those do less than justice to Wordsworth who condemn him as a turncoat to the visions of his youth. He was never this. He tempered his optimism without compromising his belief. His earliest dream of human regeneration remained his latest too. It was the ultimate basis of all his lifelong seclusion and communing with simple men in whom the virtues of a true democracy resided, the democracy of labour and of law, of faith and of resignation.

This then was Wordsworth's testament, as it must be of every poet who combines a creative desire with a critical intelligence, of all indeed who, wishing to attach to life itself the positive harmony of art, find misery and discord a contradiction and a curse. He believed

> That a benignant spirit was abroad
> Which might not be withstood, that poverty
> Abject as this would in a little time
> Be found no more, that we should see the earth
> Unthwarted in her wish to recompense
> The meek, the lowly, patient child of toil,
> All institutes for ever blotted out
> That legalised exclusion, empty pomp
> Abolished, sensual state and cruel power,
> Whether by edict of the one or few;
> And finally, as sum and crown of all,
> Should see the people having a strong hand
> In framing then our laws: whence better days
> To all mankind.

Wordsworth's belief represented an honest idealisation of the economy which he saw functioning in
Nature. He never, as Shelley, confused the natural
fact with its interpretation in human terms. It was
not any actual state of nature which he urged men to
emulate, but the principles to be drawn by human
intelligence from the physical working of the universe.
Nature obtains her creative harmony by the healthy
balance of forces, in which the physically robust
triumph. She offers her creatures the liberty both
to survive and to perish. To man liberty is no less
desirable, but such a form of it as assures the realisation of spiritual values, of those joys of conscious
harmony between man and his fellows, between
the claims of reason and instinct, of which the human
body is only the humble receptacle. And to attain
this harmony as Wordsworth said, it is necessary to
translate the material economy of force into an ideal
one of love:

> I felt
> That 'mid the loud distractions of the world
> A sovereign voice subsists within the soul, . . .
> That nothing hath a natural right to last
> But equity and reason.

This was not the "Reason" of Godwin,—that
mathematical system, which so many young minds
of that generation welcomed at first, maintaining
that only false law and dead custom and entrenched
tyranny prevented the true goodness of human
nature from realising itself, and that with the

o

removal of these obstacles and the institution of Godwin's system, all would be well. That abstract and mechanical " Reason " was found but a futile instrument either to direct to the heights the noblest instincts of man or to restrain the basest, to define " original virtue " or to confound " original vice." Its inadequacy had been discovered after the " Terror " and the invasion of Switzerland which followed. It was proved as barren of power, as it was alien to the nature of man. An enlightened view of what " Liberty " implied in a world slowly emerging from barbarism embraced something very different from this.

The equity to which Wordsworth returns again and again is a Reason which has its basis in the nature of things, a combination alike of generous instinct and prudent experience. It was a faculty of creative perception, neither abstract nor logically exact, but as indubitably real and positive as life itself, since it was not only spiritually absolute but recognised the relativity of human conditions. It provided man both with guidance in his immediate activities and with an assurance alike of an ultimate as of an immanent eternity. Wordsworth would have agreed with Schiller that " Reason is but an instrument; it is for the energy of the will and the ardour of feeling to carry it out," and that " Truth has failed so far, not for lack of wisdom, but because the heart remained closed to it, and instinct did not

act with it." For it is creative reason, combining
the virtues of thought and of feeling, that alone can
appreciate the ideal nature of things, however humble,
and measure their reality in a spiritual common-
wealth. Such a vision judges all activities and institutions beneficent so far as they give expression
to the creative instinct of man, both indvidually
and collectively. Before it all pomps and prejudices
disappear. It looks as critically upon the false
pleasures of plutocracy as on the miseries which
they entail for others, and

> With feelings of fraternal love
> Upon the unassuming things that hold
> A silent station in this beauteous world.

That alone is false to life and unworthy of perpetuation which denies the spirit expression, whether it
be a social system or a private habit. Custom
degrades the soul when it ceases to be a vital expression of humanity, and represents only a formula
of conduct or belief passively accepted. For then

> Men become bowed
> Under a growing weight of vulgar sense,
> And substitute a universe of death
> For that which moves with light and life informed,
> Actual, divine, and true.

The true man is he who, with the innocence of the
child and the conscious faculties of the man, is ever
unsubdued " by the regular action of the world."

No poet has ever had a more constant and mystical
apprehension than Wordsworth of the spirit of life

immanent in all things, but clouded or transparent according as matter resists or submits to its pure embodiment. Beauty was to him that condition of being in which this essential life shone the most vividly, and the spirit and the form were wholly one; while ugliness was either a mere negation of light, a material barrier interposing between the innate song of life and its desired utterance, or an active discord, when the particulars of a physical world, vitalised but misdirected, made war upon each other, and destroyed alike the divine and the natural unity into which they should actively merge. Such was " the busy dance Of things that pass away " which he contrasted with " a temperate show of objects that endure," and such he thought should stir in the compassionate heart of every true man not indignation but " pity for the unsightly and the violent."

Perhaps there is no more overwhelming description in his poetry of that revelation of universal power and reason conjoined, which he saw in all actuality, from the humblest flower or inanimate stone to the most glorious spectacle which nature or man can offer, than that passage in *The Prelude*, which records a majestic scene in the Alps, where

> Tumult and peace, the darkness and the light
> Were all like workings of one mind, the features
> Of the same face, blossoms upon one tree;
> Characters of the great Apocalypse,
> The types and symbols of Eternity.

He was indeed more seer than artist: it was the
essential truth in nature, the deepest feeling in man
for which he hungered with a grand impatience of
form as form.

> The surfaces of artificial life
> I neither knew nor cared for.

In the greatest art, as in the eternal moments of life,
the form fades from consciousness, because it reveals
so exactly and so potently the idea. The finite is
become the servant of the infinite, and we forget
the fact in the truth. To Wordsworth this ideal
was not remote; it pervaded the actual world, was
in it and under it and above it like a force of elec-
tricity. He discerned it and trembled to it, as to a
" sentiment of being," which bound him to all life
in a deep mysterious brotherhood. There was
possibly something of the elder brother in his attitude.
He felt his responsibility towards life no less than
his ecstasy in her activities. He longed to help all
things to know themselves in absolute truth, to cast
off artificialities and sluggishness and irrationality,
to be free and proud in the simple certainty of living
to the full, and guaranteeing to others a kindred life
in the order of ideal nature.

> To every natural form, rock, fruit, or flower,
> Even the loose stones that cover the high way,
> I gave a moral life: I saw them feel,
> Or linked them to some feeling.

Wordsworth believed that all inanimate nature

shared, if to an infinitely less degree, the consciousness of life which man variously possesses.

> And 'tis my faith that every flower
> Enjoys the air it breathes.

He never claimed with Coleridge that " in our life
alone does nature live ": he was too absolute a
mystic and too instinctive an Evolutionist for that.
All his individual sensations he felt to be but particular vibrations in one organic note, to which it
was the duty of all to contribute what of life and
music they had in them, and so swell the volume of
the music and enrich it.   Man to him was both a
sensitive and a creative being; if he ceased to be
the one, it mattered not which, he lost also the
faculty for being the other . . .

> Thou must give
> Else never canst receive.

For he knew that without perception a poet cannot truly imagine, and without imagination he
cannot truly perceive.

It was this ideal reciprocity between all living
things, this sympathetic expressiveness, which seemed
to him the only quality necessary to happiness or
certain to create on Earth " one great Society " in
which man lived both in vital harmony with his
neighbour and with the phenomenal universe.
Naturally such a view of essential principles led
Wordsworth to attack, and with justice, many of the
pretensions of conventional education, books, too,

written to display the pyrotechnics of the mind, or the prejudice of the " few " who saw life only from the rich man's or the scholar's standpoint; as also the exclusively analytical tendency of science by which it multiplies distinctions rather than emphasises affinities, and so destroys man's feeling for the unity of things.

The same motive underlay his attack on formal poetic diction and the use of supernatural artifice to convey visionary or transcendental truths. Nature to him was sufficiently a miracle to render all such devices superfluous, and apt to distort vision rather than clarify it. The language of the heavens and the earth and of human life in its infinite variability, was enough to convey to him wonders untold. The craving for the unusual and marvellous was one of the earliest symptoms in men of a desire to escape the oppression of fact, even by surrendering the senses or the fancy to fiction. To describe or invent some region of which man has no knowledge, or to recall a mediæval period, strange by lapse of time, was one of the commonest delights of Romanticism. All that is unaccustomed or alien to our common experience has at least the virtue of liberating us from the routine of material existence and encouraging an unprejudiced acceptance of the strange and sensational. But such devices may easily be abused or may only startle without enlightening, and to Wordsworth, who saw inspired truth enough in simple fact rightly apprehended, it seemed that a craving for the spectacular must and should give way to a "strengthening love for things that we have seen." The exaggerations of Romanticism should only serve to prepare man for the ideal revelations of naturalism. And by the side of Coleridge's *Ancient Mariner* we have Wordsworth's *Peter Bell*, which, although incomparably inferior in pure imagination and lyrical power, chiefly perhaps because written in conscious illustration of a doctrine, shows that fact may be as strange and surprising as fancy, and that to simple minds the natural may prove more supernatural than the magical. But Wordsworth justified his principle most emphatically when most unconsciously clothing what might seem trivial incidents with mystic illumination, as in that vivid description of the place where a murderer had once been hung and how he saw

> A girl who bore a pitcher on her head,
> And seemed with difficult steps to force her way
> Against the blowing wind. It was in truth
> An ordinary sight; but I should need
> Colours and words that are unknown to man
> To paint the visionary dreariness.

Or again:

> 'Tis a common tale,
> An ordinary sorrow of man's life,
> A tale of silent suffering, hardly clothed
> In bodily form.

The life of man stripped of all external forms and viewed intimately " whether by words, looks, sighs,

or tears revealed," must excite in every man of un-
dulled sensibility and human tenderness as inexhaustible a wonder as nature does in the heart of
the child. It was these essential values which Wordsworth prized, the central tragedies and ecstasies of
human feelings brought into conflict with hard
Necessity, of manhood triumphing against desperate
odds, or womanhood suffering without complaint
the bitterness and desolation of an evil destiny. He
saw the whole world " As it appears to unaccustomed
eyes," Nature as the interpreter of awful and benign
powers, and man as the index of a divine mind
struggling for perfect and conscious expression. For

> Whether we be young or old,
> Our destiny, our being's heart and home,
> Is with infinitude, and only there.

Inevitably therefore he was scornful of all empty
forms or cultivated insincerities, which prevented
that process of " drinking-in the soul of things,"
that passionate intuition whereby the instinctive
creature apprehends the eternal truths which govern
and enrich all living things. This was what he meant
by moral strength—an intercourse with the absolute
through the relative in contradistinction with the
conventional morality of men, which is an artificial,
if historical code, representing only the relative
standards of the time, and compromising truth in
the interests of class or social utility. To a poet
forms and conventions are only valuable so far as

they embody a living idea.   Wordsworth found this idea most vital and most in correspondence with the necessity of this earth, as well as with the aspiration of man, in nature herself, and in a simple peasant class.   For both were immemorial, and, as it were, slowly evolved from a chaos of darkness and primæval storm.   He was too sane to accept, as many of his contemporaries did, in their enthusiastic aspiration, the easy sensational dream, which disregarded natural necessity and visioned an ideal superhuman life.   Consequently much of his poetry loses in rapture for what it gains in truth to actuality.   It is ideal within the limits of mortality; it is moral because it admits not only the divine soul in man, but the poor earthly casket in which the soul is lodged.

Thus, although no poet for the last hundred years has written words more passionately removed by choice and rhythm from the level of prose than Wordsworth, or laboured more painstakingly after exact observance and that corroboration of the idea by the fact which is the creed of science, yet none has more obstinately condemned in language and thought every taint of falsity, whether found in the use of habitual instead of original terminology, of tricks of phrasing and ornamental conceits, instead of the choice and inevitable speech of sincere emotion, or in the material complaisance of science with her dull eye " chained to its object in brute slavery." Indeed he prided himself on being " shy and un-

practised in the strife of phrase." Everything which
prevented the expression of a man's whole self, or
developed one of his faculties at the cost of another,
was to him a cause of stumbling. A man, he urged,
cannot learn the truth of life, and so live in active
love with all things, if he depends on either mind or
instinct alone. The heavens and earth, man and his
many tongues, and the books into which he has
poured his thought, are only " under-agents " of a
divine spirit, scrolls insignificant but for the idea of
life which they should convey. Education to him was
only worthy when it prepared youth for that kinship
with life, enriching instinct and reason together, and
teaching men to see everywhere the reality beyond
the fact, to feel an enraptured communion with all
things that are.   It was thus that for Wordsworth

> The lonely roads
> Were open schools in which I daily read
> With most delight the passions of mankind.

3

To this mystical vision of a benign spirit, immanent
in nature and in the heart of man, Wordsworth
came by a difficult road, a road of spiritual warfare
and dejection. We see him in his youth elated with
hope; next shocked by experience into a bleak and
barren despondency; then in the full summer of
his strength, " happy and quiet in his cheerfulness,"
blessed with a " natural graciousness of mind "; and

lastly solitary, sententious, and prematurely aged, murmuring to himself as he walks the country roads,

> Neither slow nor eager: but unmoved,
> And with a quiet uncomplaining voice,
> A stately air of mild indifference.

And stirred by an impulse in which pity and tedium combine, we are tempted to repeat his own words:

> It doth not seek the cold:
> This neither is its courage nor its choice,
> But its necessity in being old.

Yet Wordsworth's spiritual history is profoundly enlightening. He alone of the great poets of his age lived long enough to complete it: and if the poet in him surrendered at last to the moraliser, it was not before reconciling while still a poet his vision of truth with that of beauty. We are indeed too apt to bank the fire of Wordsworth's youth, as he did himself, in the ashes of his old age. Few can have been more radiantly instinctive than he as boy and youth. Life was then to him a source of active animal pleasure; urgently he knew the sheer unreflective joy of existence. And later, when he first began consciously to consider his sensations, it was Nature for her own sake which he prized, the mere fact of an inviting world, beautiful, stormy, and tremulously alive:

> A passion, she,
> A rapture often, and immediate love
> Ever at hand.

Time was far yet from bringing the philosophic

mind: the loveliness and the terror of life were enough to satisfy with wonder and awe. He drank at the fountain of life, as a tree stretching out its leaves to catch the dew.

> I held unconscious intercourse with beauty
> Old as creation, drinking in a pure
> Organic pleasure from the silver wreaths
> Of curling mist, or from the level plain
> Of waters coloured by impending clouds.

The political and social ferment of the French Revolution translated this uncritical ecstasy into human terms:

> But Nature then was sovereign in my mind,
> And mighty forms, seizing a youthful fancy,
> Had given a charter to irregular hopes.

He hoped and believed that man was about to realise at a leap that universal harmony which he saw in nature. Failing in his young impatience to consider the means by which nature attained her harmony, he disregarded too the arguments in human nature against man's sudden conversion from slavery or bigotry to a life of reason and grace.

It was the common error of all the enthusiastic minds of that generation. Rebellion coloured their creative desire with sensational exaggeration. They believed too easily in the possibility of miracles, and underestimated the logic of fact.

The distinctive feature, however, of Wordsworth is that the disillusionment which inevitably followed

such a disregard of actuality, such a confusion
between what is and what ought to be, did not
excite in him as in others a spirit either of personal
arrogance, cynicism, or self-pity. It filled him with
a profound pessimism for a time; it sent him on
long journeys of thought and enquiry as to where
the error lay which had led to such a catastrophe
of hope: it humbled and jaded him, and to a degree
tamed him, but the result was eventually an added
illumination, more tranquil perhaps and less dazzling
than the " light that never was, on sea or land,"
but more constant, satisfying and enriching.

Wordsworth's grief after his return from France
was traceable to a private as well as to a public
cause. Something of his unhappy private passion
he has described in *Vaudracour and Julia*,—there
are references to it also in *The Prelude*, and in many
poems devoted to the theme of forsaken maidens,
such as *The Ruined Cottage* or *Her Eyes are Wild*.
It is enough to say that he had loved ardently and,
in the face of opposition, transgressed the conventional moral code, the marriage-service of respectability, signifying thereby as he says, " Nature's
rebellion against monstrous laws." The union,
however, had ended sadly; authority and circumstance had prevented the legalising or continuance
of the relationship. Wordsworth's Love, Hope, and
humanitarian desire therefore, his instinct for
liberty, and his intuition of universal truth, received

two severe and even staggering rebuffs during and after his stay in France. He saw what he had believed to be beneficent powers and fraternal enthusiasms degenerating into lusts and bloodshed; and in his own intimate experience he had learnt how inflexible could be the tyranny of circumstance. And when at last he heard that his own country had declared war on France, his whole being received a shock which it with difficulty survived. It threw him " out of the pale of love," " soured and corrupted, upwards to the source " his sentiments, and for a time he lost all conviction in a maze of distraction and despair.

> I had raised a pyre
> Upon the basis of the coming time,
> That fell in ruins round me.

It was now " amid a melancholy waste of hopes o'erthrown " that the lesson which he had learnt unconsciously from nature, that example which she offers of enduring consistency, stood him in good stead. He was too deeply passionate a man to turn querulous, too honest-minded to avoid the problem and find satisfaction in his own independent egotism. He had to fight his way out into the light, or perish silently, so far as he was a sentient being, in the dark. His only hope was to suffer and be strong.

It was indeed a time of testing. But the trial was necessary for the vindication of truth. Wordsworth

had generalised instinctively about both nature and
man, and the world, as is its custom, had apparently
shown his speculations and ardours to be amiable
nonsense, had torn his faith to shreds and humbled
his pride as a man. To one so honest with himself
it was impossible to continue writing poetry at all
if it was in truth only the fantastic creation of his
own desire, unrelated to things as they actually
were. Many a lesser poet would not have been
troubled by the apparent contradiction; he would
not have felt the cultivation of agreeable fancy, if
it resulted in pleasing poems, to be a thing dis-
creditable either to his genius or his integrity. To
Wordsworth such a contingency was intolerable.

> Ah! what avails imagination high
> Or question deep? What profits all that earth,
> Or heaven's blue vault, is suffered to put forth
> Of impulse or allurement. . . .
> If nowhere
> A habitation, for consummate good,
> Or for progressive virtue, by the search
> Can be attained?

His sense of responsibility to man, of all that he
shared with his fellows, was as strong as his
elemental instinct, his responsiveness to the creative force of life. The two had to be reconciled,
if he was to escape being torn between desire
and disappointment.

To him poetry was a real interpretation of life:
and any honest labour was preferable to a mere

gratification of the self by idle fantasies or airy speculations. He conceived it incumbent on him therefore to prove the truth of his vision and of his imaginative ideal, or admit failure and defeat. For

> By the storms of circumstance unshaken,
> And subject neither to eclipse nor wane,
> Duty exists.

He tried himself by two methods: firstly he descended from the universal to the particular; he examined life in the small as earnestly as he had rapturously surrendered to it in the large. He had known and was to know again more powerfully " his godlike hours," and felt

> What an empire we inherit
> As natural beings in the strength of nature,

but for the time the disastrous spectacle of human conduct led him to distrust principalities and powers. His love of truth was too wide and deep a passion ever to tempt him into the arid fields of casuistry, but he realised that

> Wisdom is oft-time nearer when we stoop
> Than when we soar,

that only by examining individuals, those too who were true offspring of nature, reared amid simple surroundings, far from artificial fashions or affected culture, and tutored by the realities of labouring life, could he discover whether his spontaneous

P

exultation in nature was justified, whether it was
a mere personal sensation or an intuition of absolute
truth. He descended from the mountain-tops and
walked the country lanes, not only to examine and
enquire of each man, woman or child,

> Where many a sheltered and well-tended plant
> Bears, on the humblest ground of social life,
> Blossoms of piety and innocence,

but to make every stone, tree and flower an object
of close and penetrating contemplation, each figuring
in his mind as witness for or against his own too
ardent principles, now brought to judgment. Yet
perhaps his own description of this life as a favourite
school is the better. For henceforth Wordsworth
never relinquished his effort to learn, and too often
to teach. The poet became the pupil, and the pupil
ended by being the pedagogue. A study of life in
detail relieved him of his doubt, and confirmed
his faith with sound evidence, but the habit of
enquiry and disquisition, rather than of complete
surrender to an experience, still clung to him, after
the need of conscious criticism had ceased to exist,
and when indeed by its perpetuation it only impeded
his creative faculties.

The second test to which Wordsworth submitted
his genius encouraged this tendency, for he enlarged
it into a principle. It is contained in his own dictum
that " poetry takes its origin from emotion recollected
in tranquillity," a truth dependent at least on the

poet's capacity to select only those emotions which were originally passionate enough to justify and reward recollection, and at the same time to renew themselves with all the added depth and mellowness which an intermediate absorption should guarantee.

Wordsworth erred in both these directions. He distrusted immediate instinct, because it had deluded him with exaggerated hopes and reduced him to such despair, and he believed that by retrospection he would be able to attain all the inevitability of passion, while purging it of any falsehood inherent in immediate sensation. Often enough he succeeded in this, and we find, notably in the *Lines composed a few Miles above Tintern Abbey* and in many of his shorter lyrics, such as *The Solitary Reaper*, *Stepping Westward* or *She was a Phantom of Delight*, both the original experience recalled in all its pure vividness, and interwoven with it the ideal reality of which it was an image, invoked by contemplation and enriched by the kindred associations which have gathered round it during the period that it had lain fertilising in the memory. The same process makes the stories which he drew from the lives of humble human beings so memorable, such for example as *The Affliction of Margaret*. It is not merely the poignant realism of a human history which moves us, but the universalising of the tale by Wordsworth himself, who has made it a part of his own great tenderness, and clothed it in the images of a mind

brooding long over man's destiny, and on those
elemental passions

> Essential and eternal in the heart,
> That, 'mid the simpler forms of rural life,
> Exist more simple in their elements,
> And speak a plainer language.

This passing from the immediate experience into
solemn thought, into an intense and lingering
contemplation, Wordsworth has described many
times. After meditation the actual scene or the
momentary incident returned to him, not only
freed of all insignificant detail, but related to the
consciousness which he possessed of absolute life.
In such a condition of trance he felt like Peter Bell,

> As if his mind were sinking deep
> Through years that have been long asleep!

The new sensation took its place among those others
which had preceded it, and which had also been
thus spiritually purified. Imagination to him was,
as we have said, a combination of the passive and
active faculties, of perception and creation. The
senses accepted and retained the impression, for
the reason to test in its vital and discriminating
fire, until nothing but the pure gold within the
impression survived for poetry to present. This
slow and tranquil contemplation was to Wordsworth
as much sensuous as intellectual; indeed it was as
if he prolonged and retarded what is customarily
an immediate physical reaction to a material stimulus,

that he might both continue to enjoy the sensation and enquire into its nature, as:

> Oh then, the calm
> And dead still water lay upon my mind
> Even with a weight of pleasure.

Or again:

> And deep feelings had impressed
> So vividly great objects that they lay
> Upon his mind like substances, whose presence
> Perplexed the bodily sense.

Many critics from the time of De Quincey have imputed the changed quality noticeable in almost all Wordsworth wrote after the crisis of his dejection to a failure of animal energy, to the rapid ravages of a too ardent temperament that consumed itself in its own fires. Others have thought that he never recovered from the shock which his instincts received, and so henceforth went reluctantly to meet sensation, with a tract too in his hand, and a homily ready prepared. Both of these we think are partial explanations of the change.

Wordsworth had, to begin with, advanced on truth too hastily for his reason to master it, and paid the penalty by a blow which for a time rendered him almost senseless. He groped his way back, and after time had healed his wounds, though the scars remained, he advanced again with caution, but with ever-growing confidence and exultation. Certainly the early disaster and the throw-back which it entailed impeded the organic development of his genius, and induced him sometimes to choose the lower but the safer path rather than the dangerous heights where there was little foothold, and immediate instinct was the only guide against a false step. Particularly is this true of his attitude towards sexual love. Circumstance had conspired that he should experience it to his hurt and henceforth he went in dread of it. Here alone convention may be said to have defeated him. For love is as imperfectly realised by the man who fears it as by him who is " passion's slave." But elsewhere he was troubled by an imaginative rather than a physical dilemma. It was a question whether he could trust his imagination to be, in the first wild moment of instinctive apprehension, both "absolute power," "clearest insight," "amplitude of mind" and "Reason in her most exalted mood." There were times when the elemental forces of life broke in upon his studiousness with all their old intolerance and terror,

> Like the noise of wolves
> Howling in troops upon the Bothnic main.

Or:

> Like living men, moved slowly through the mind
> By day, and were a trouble to my dream.

His response, both physical and spiritual, to the primal power of nature, whether in its savage or its beneficent aspect, never failed. Indeed he more than once confesses that he loved the beauty " which hath terror in it," and elsewhere he wrote:

> Oh! what a joy it were, in vigorous health,
> To have a body (this our vital frame
> With shrinking sensibility endued,
> And all the nice regards of flesh and blood)
> And to the elements surrender it
> As if it were a spirit!

It was rather human nature, with its aspirations and its tenacity, its credulous daring and its weak foolishness, which he henceforth approached tentatively, deprecating those raptures and agitations of the sense that had brought on him and others the darkness of disillusionment. He separated wisely a human from a cosmic dispensation:

> Obedient to the strong creative power
> Of human passion. Sympathies there are
> More tranquil, yet perhaps of kindred birth,
> That steal upon the meditative mind,
> And grow with thought.

Of man he always spoke now " with somewhat of a solemn tone." He had seen how hard human life was materially for millions, spiritually for all; he had learnt the folly of putting his trust in speedy panaceas. The removal of misery from human lives was to prove a long, perhaps endless process. From the oppression of that knowledge he could only escape by doing something himself to alleviate by understanding the fact of human pain. He could only lighten his own burden by shouldering that of others; and so when he communed with man as distinct from nature, it was to sing

> Some philosophic song
> Of truth that cherishes our daily life.

The truth of human life can only be discovered through self-effacing sympathy, and thus to the masculine faculty which was so eminently his, the love of battle and great storms and wide prospects, and the power of disciplined thought, he added the feminine sensibility with which he walked meekly penitent, gentle and enquiring in the presence of simple human lives, and of minute natural activities, until amid " all the sweetness of a common dawn " the lamb and the lamb's mother and their tender ways were enough to touch him to the heart, the flower to fill him with thoughts, that lie " too deep for tears."

4

Wordsworth, then, did not suddenly sacrifice genius to didacticism; rather he changed the direction and conformation of his powers, while sometimes the control he exercised over them was arbitrary and mistaken. An apprehension of the universal always remained with him, but more and more his surrender to it became a moral as well as a natural act. His reason intruded upon an instinctive experience, and that consciously. No sensation was now accepted merely for the pleasure it gave; it found its place in an entire philosophy of life. Sometimes the sensation was too weak to survive assimilation. The philosophy which Wordsworth had abstracted from a thousand previous experiences crushed the life out of it, and the complacent maxim enjoyed another vain repetition. Or again it happened that Wordsworth in his reaction from airy speculation to actual things, however minute, put too implicit a trust " in the eye of him who passes me," and repeated incidents of human life which were too trivial or pedestrian in themselves to justify selection, and which interested not the poet in him so much as the curious enquirer into " those human sentiments that make this earth so dear." The expression of such facts was inevitably as tame as the facts themselves. For they were not intense enough to awaken even in his mystical mind, " for ever voyaging through strange seas of Thought alone," the pulse of passion or the warmth of sentiment. And so being unprovocative of life, they encouraged all the secondary platitudes which lurk in a poet's mind as reflections of his idealistic desire. These descents into prose were the price which he paid for insisting that he should be sure of his feet however high he climbed. But when the incident deserved his attention, and the experience moved him so deeply that his whole being was caught up into it, his thought steeped in feeling, then indeed he and we reap the reward of his devout honesty of purpose. We hear a tone richer and profounder than instinct alone in its wildest and sublimest moment can compass, the voice alike of the eternal sea and the eternal man.

> Far and wide the clouds were touched
> And in their silent faces could be read
> Unutterable love. Sound needed none,
> Nor any voice of joy; his spirit drank
> The spectacle: sensation, soul, and form
> All melted in him; they swallowed up
> His animal being; in them did he live,
> And by them did he live; they were his life.
> In such access of mind, in such high hour
> Of visitation from the living God,
> Thought was not; in enjoyment it expired.

This is both moral and elemental, and it was Wordsworth's achievement to unite the two, to balance an absolute and abstract imagination which would destroy the order of the world, by a reason which emphasised the law of necessity.

5

Wordsworth's contemporaries worshipped nature, only to find her false. He alone, surviving temporary disillusionment, kept his faith with her, and proved her true. It was a singular performance, and had the generation which succeeded him studied his naturalism as persistently as they cultivated the many spurious elements in Romanticism, both mankind and art would have benefited. There would have been less private horticulture, and more real and catholic achievement, more sanity and joy. For though Wordsworth may have been " a meditative, oft a suffering man," though at times he may have seemed sad "at thought of raptures now for ever flown," it was always joy which he expressed, the joy of the sane man who has traced all misfortune to its source, who cannot suffer any fatal reversal of belief or expectation because he knows and accepts the cause of things, but who in his ecstatic kinship with life knows "that love sublime, . . . that strength of feeling great above all human estimate."

He retained his delight in nature primarily because he had the insight to distinguish the inanimate from the human world. Nature taught him truth because he was able to interpret her as a man. Her fact served his intelligence, and her processes, however brutal, were found to have an ideal correspondence in humanity. Translated into human terms, she was worthy of admiration and imitation; so far as man accepted her materially, so far as he allowed her to make him an animal, she was detestable. Wordsworth realised the distinction between idealism and realism, and how the one should blossom from the other, and by this ascertained path won to nature's ideal liberty, dismissing her real, methodical licence from his mind as a trivial rather than a terrifying thing. And so in the strength of that vision he could say:

> One adequate support
> For the calamities of mortal life
> Exists—one only; an assured belief

> That the procession of our fate, howe'er
> Sad or disturbed, is ordered by a Being
> Of infinite benevolence and power.

This was no weak fatalism, or that convenient placid faith which for many excellent and inoffensive souls takes the place of individual effort. It was the result of a long process of testing life with all the mechanical accuracy of the scientist, and all the synthetic faculty of the philosopher, and all the emotional sympathy of the poet. With him as with Peter Bell the spirits of the Mind had usurped " upon the rights of visual sense," and by studying nature at her work, from the meanest flower up to the highest human intelligence, he had satisfied himself that a beneficent spirit did indeed lie behind all her activities, a spirit of law, indifferently cruel on the lower planes of existence, and against which none could in safety rebel: but a spirit also of life, aspiring ever upward through unconsciousness to consciousness and liberty. He, like Shelley and Keats, discovered ideally the principle of Evolution, and so could view all nature with a joy more assured than that which he tasted in the abandonment of youth and unreflecting passion.

> Happy is he who lives to understand,
> Not human nature only, but explores
> All natures,—to the end that he may find
> The law that governs each; and where begins
> The union, the partition where, that makes
> Kind and degree, among all visible Beings;
> The constitutions, powers, and faculties
> Which they inherit,—cannot step beyond,—

> And cannot fall beneath; that do assign
> To every class its station and its office.
> Through all the mighty commonwealth of things;
> Up from the creeping plant to sovereign Man.
> Such converse, if directed by a meek,
> Sincere, and humble spirit, teaches love:
> For knowledge is delight; and such delight
> Breeds love.

The theories, of which Darwin and Einstein have later given practical demonstration, are here innate in the absolute vision of Wordsworth himself. For in him the spirit of Science rectified the errors of Romanticism, while that of Poetry universalised the logic of mind. Yet though he found nature in her aim, as distinct from her means, to be good, he did not surrender himself blindly to her impulse, or presuppose the joys of a sensational Paradise. For this reason many who prefer in poetry an easy and sentimental consolation, an escape from fact rather than a transcending of it, have derided Wordsworth's moral tone, as if it implied an acceptance of half-truths of secondary rather than ultimate values. Wordsworth's occasional moralising deserves such criticism, but not his basic morality. He was too genuine a man to desert for long the world as it is in the pursuit of personal ecstasy. Indeed he found, as all men must who would live honourably, that in art as well as life there was no justification for a purely egotistic attitude. The life around him, even in its cruelty and squalor, had to be met fairly and reconciled with his desires. Yet only a true, as

distinct from an artificial life, deserved to be held
in the balances. For all else was unreal, and only the
more dead, for its simulation of life and brilliancy.
But Nature and natural men were the fruit of life
as he himself was, and them he could not overlook.
These then he studied, and he found first that
although the economy of nature was built upon
physical warfare, the result was a system of mutual
dependency, to which each element alike contributed
according to its peculiar characteristics. To this
creative end every other consideration was by
Nature sacrificed. The vegetable and animal worlds
lived by law, crude but impartial: and this law was
the physical symbol of love. For love is creative
desire, which yearns always to produce the intensest
harmony, and so the most beautiful form of life.
In short, mind showed itself in nature as the organisa-
tion of forces for the best physical ends, in man for
the highest spiritual. Humanity was a world of pure
force seeking to become a world of pure intelligence.

Wordsworth satisfied himself therefore that the
natural world was in its method brutal, in its expression beautiful, and in its principle moral. It was an
organism in which the self-expression of every unit
was intense, and of which the synthesis was harmony.
Wherever he looked he saw consistency, energy and
submission to discipline. The life-spirit which
inspired this world was therefore beneficent, because
it was absolutely creative.

Thou dost preserve the stars from wrong
And the most ancient heavens, through Thee, are fresh and strong.

There was destruction, but rarely, if ever, waste; the humble bird which perished beneath the talons of the hawk served a life-purpose as veritably as the hawk itself. Man too had sprung from this natural soil, and as a physical being shared the instincts of the creature, but to him belonged also the directing intelligence of a creator. In the majority of men the creative spirit was still dormant, or darkened by unreasoned animal desires, and Wordsworth saw that the only certain way of happiness lay in a development of man's reasoning powers, combined with a close fidelity to nature's principles. Man would thus be an ideal being in his pursuit of rational rather than physical values, and a natural one by his sympathy with the creative instinct which he shared with all living things.

It is because Wordsworth emphasised the limitations under which man lived that he has been accused of moral compromise as a poet. For a poet to guess at heaven in disregard of earth was to him as unallowable as for a man to abandon his reason in the pursuit of sensation. Life to him was inevitably a compromise between absolute freedom of mind and the limitations of necessity. By studying nature man would learn the lessons of self-sacrifice, endurance, duty and joy, which she reveals in fact; but by virtue of his mind he would transcend the coarseness and excess upon which her economy is built.

> Be taught, O faithful Consort, to control
> Rebellious passion: for the Gods approve
> The depth, and not the tumult, of the soul;
> A fervent, not ungovernable love.

The passive loyalty of the creature to the processes of life is illustrated in " Peter Bell's " ass, or the fidelity of the Shepherd's dog, or in the spectacle of the White Doe of Rylstone, who in the midst of overwhelming adversity remains unmoved and calm. In the creature such endurance is of course instinctive, in man it must be consciously practised, until it becomes, as Wordsworth shows it in the character of the Happy Warrior or the Leech Gatherer, a natural habit of disinterestedness, and an ever renewed sense of the value and interdependence of life. Wordsworth saw that men could only attain this spiritual tranquillity and catholic sympathy through accepting law as well as desiring Liberty, and his creed is perhaps formulated at its best in his *Ode to Duty*, in which he cries that serenity and happiness can only come to those who admit life to be a stern Lawgiver as well as a benignant Grace, who draw on her for strength, but bow also to her discipline, who are free because they have ordered their steps by the evidence of her processes, through which alone can shine in certainty the light of her truth.   The visionary splendour and the prosaic fact were to him, as to every great mystic, always commingled.

> An intermingling of Heaven's pomp is spread
> On ground which British shepherds tread.

It was thus that he strengthened his own resolution, and resumed in middle-age the faith of his youth, deepened and secured by rational verification. He saw that men went equally wrong when they surrendered their humanity to nature's physical licence, as when they allowed their selfish egotism to deny nature instead of transcending her. Even the birds could teach these latter a better way:

> With Nature never do they wage
> A foolish strife; they see
> A happy youth, and their old age
> Is beautiful and free.

Yet Wordsworth never encouraged, as so many disciples of Rousseau, a weak surrender of human will to uncriticised instinct.

> Here must thou be, O man!
> Power to thyself; no helper hast thou here.

He knew that it was not by slavish subservience to nature's method, but by continuous communion with her spirit, of which the physical world is only an index, that mankind could learn to live creatively without sacrificing his human birthright. They could only safely desert nature's fact by ascending to her idea. Though such communion with all the forces of life striving after absolute expression,

Q

all the loveliness, for example, mirrored in a countryside, may enter into human consciousness uncon-
ditionally, and mould the very features of the
initiate. In such lines as the following, the maiden
has become as surely part of nature as the words that
describe the rivulets have the motion of the stream:

> The stars of midnight shall be dear
> To her; and she shall lean her ear
> In many a secret place
> Where rivulets dance their wayward round,
> And beauty born of murmuring sound
> Shall pass into her face.

It is the idea of nature, of which the phenomenal
world is only the transient form, that, playing perpetually upon human sensibility, can so transform
the matter of life. Man can thus drink of life at the
source without intoxication, and complete his one-
ness with the creative spirit that pervades " with
its own divine vitality " both the " forest-tree " and
humanity itself, without transgressing the universal
concord which is as intense an aim of life as that of
self-expression.   So only is man's mind proved
unconquerable by time, change, or apparent disappointment, because it is made one with the
creative mind itself. Of all such it may be said as
of the child of one of his most famous sonnets:

> Thou liest in Abraham's bosom all the year;
> And worshipp'st at the Temple's inner shrine,
> God being with thee when we know it not.

For Wordsworth's study of nature in her small

workings no less than his wonder at her moments
of monumental beauty, convinced him of the existence of an originating spirit, a vast prototype of the
human mind, of which the phenomenal world was
the expression. " It appeared to me," he says,

> The type
> Of a majestic intellect, its acts
> And its possessions, what it has and craves,
> What in itself it is, and would become.
> There I beheld the emblem of a mind
> That feeds upon infinity, that broods
> Over the dark abyss, intent to hear
> Its voice issuing forth to silent light
> In one continuous stream; a mind sustained
> By recognitions of transcendent power,
> In sense conducting to ideal form,
> In soul of more than mortal privilege.

To him, therefore, God was the great poet of existence, the absolute symbol of both human intellect
and instinct, the infinite creative being whose medium
was the universe, and whose desire after more perfect
expression never failed, but renewed itself from
moment to moment, and generation to generation.

It was, then, Wordsworth's distinction to reconcile,
instead of confusing, the actual and the ideal, the
phenomenal and the eternal. He was no idle dreamer
or impatient visionary. He would neither solace
himself with abstractions, nor accept the easy vicious
creed of ingenious naturalism. He knew that physical
nature, with its impulses and desires, its fiery sensuousness, its cruelty and its cunning, was the soil

upon which all purified life must grow, if it is not
to degenerate into the sterile offspring of mechanical
mind.   The physical and the rational were in him
supremely fused, until instinct was transformed into
mystical intuition.   And so natural decay, and
transient misfortune, the worldly spectacle of pain
and folly, were impotent to crush his faith.   Death
itself was only an expression of active and beneficent
life, a reason rather for confidence and exultation
than for sorrow.   As he wrote when he heard of the
expected death of Mr. Fox:

> A power is passing from the earth
> To breathless Nature's dark abyss;
> But when the great and good depart
> What is it more than this—
>
> That Man, who is from God sent forth,
> Doth yet again to God return?—
> Such ebb and flow must ever be,
> Then wherefore should we mourn?

Wordsworth believed in the innocence, not of
nature or of man, but of life. It was for man to make
of himself an instrument through which the creative
music might sound at its truest and most potent,
to see that the world of his own sensuous and
intellectual being, no less than that of men at large,
should be one in which the constructive spirit
was everywhere alive, in which instinct could taste
an uncloying exultation, being purged of every
destructive, possessive or dominating desire; and
in which thought, tamed of its pride, together with

affection and human kindness, were rather natural unlegalised attitudes than the result of prescribed conduct or conventional morality: a world which the sense of universal kinship bathed in genial sunshine, and quickened with the perpetual joy of spring.

This vision was Wordsworth's. It lacked in its purest expressions nothing in ardency, even in intoxication; but it also submitted to the conditions of this earth and the dimensions under which we live. His enthusiasm was enriched, but also chastened, by truth. To some, Wordsworth's humility as a man seems to degrade his sovereignty as a poet. Yet Wordsworth learnt that the true sovereign in poetry, as in life, is the servant of his State, not the tyrant: that an Earthly Paradise is not to be gained either by natural or supernatural anarchy, but by inspired reason, sifting all material things, and shaping out of them the living beauty which haunts with ideal suggestion each visionary mind. It was as profitless to create spirit without body, as body without spirit; the idea and the fact needed each other, whether in nature or in man, and none could safely live in the radiance of ideal beauty who did not understand the hard logic of the material world. Life therefore imposed a double obligation, neither part of which could be disregarded:

> Let good men feel the soul of nature,
> And see things as they are.

CHAPTER VIII

THE STRICKEN YEARS

Our religions and moralities have been trimmed to flatter us, till they are all emasculate and sentimentalised, and only please and weaken. Truth is of a rougher strain. In the harsh face of life faith can read a bracing gospel.—R. L. STEVENSON.

I

IT is easier to admit than to explain the spiritual nostalgia which modern taste detects so generally in Victorian literature. Many, possibly fearing infection, have preferred to dismiss the disease in summary terms rather than diagnose its intricate and particular causes. To-day, however, our criticism, if searching, should be free from the irritation of either envy or fear. Viewed generally, the Victorian age is apt to suggest a sultry, undulating plain, ignorant of either bright sunshine or unbroken cloud, with its solemnity undisturbed by lightning or its complacence by the threat of a gathering storm. Yet to assail this complacency with cynicism or irony is only to accept the condition and deplore it. It is not to understand either it or ourselves the better, which alone justifies the criticism of one age by another. Yet we are equally liable to miss the truth of an age, if, as some critics have done, we prove

too generous to intention as distinct from performance. Many writers, for example, have cited " nobleness " as the distinctive characteristic of the Victorian
age. It is true that a vague air of nobleness was
allowed in the last century, like a magniloquent
charity, to cover a multitude of sins.

There were many then who cried peace, when
there was no peace and little honour, many whose
virtue consisted in a rather mechanical blowing of
moral trumpets, in what John Mitchel called " this
triumphant glorification of a current century upon
being the century it is." We suspect that men took
life sententiously, because they dared not live it to
the full in all its delight and passion and humour,
that they wished to mean something for lack of
being something, that their moral purpose was
stronger than their logic, and that so their actions
were often, without intention, unjust, foolish, and
to our mind exasperating. Life had become more
of a material institution than a spiritual experience,
and the structure was always interposing disastrously
between man and his natural desire, the secondary
and conditional value encroaching on the essential,
so that everywhere we detect behind a spacious
and conventional calm the irritation of healthy
instincts suppressed and turned into artificial
channels. We look in fact almost in vain in the
literature of these years for that true nobility of a
mind at peace with itself and master of all circum-

stance, for large and simple utterance and devoted finish, and for matter worthy of the style; or for such high, pure, intellectual beauty as Spenser worshipped in an earlier age. Rather over this period so apparently prosperous and earnest and creative there hung a continual threat of sleeping sickness, by which even the finest spirits were infected, and to which the weaker gradually succumbed.

Yet an ethical view of art and of life is not obsolete, as some critics have too hastily supposed, provided the ethic be a true and not a partial one, provided it represent a passion for all things fair and vital and never lapse into the unhealthy habit common to timid people, of preaching disquisitions and loving blackguards at a distance for providing them with a text. Circumstances beyond their control begot the Victorian dilemma; the seeds of their misfortune were sown before the nineteenth century began, and it would be as foolish as ungrateful to despise a disease which is assuredly the condition of any health to which we may pretend. In a recent survey of this period, Professor Elton asks rather pertinently whence this malady came: " From the long stagnant peace, which furnished no rallying point in action for the national soul? or from the exhaustion following on a sanguine inventive epoch? or from over exoticism of sympathy? or from the habit of introspection, which at such a period gains ground, or from what? " To all of these solutions we may agree without any risk of error, and yet all of them can with much justice be referred to one source,—and that the interpretation of Rousseau in England by the Romantic movement. The French Revolution in its vague call to liberty and its emphasis of individual will is comparable to the Reformation as a world-shaking movement. The whole of life was suddenly revealed to man's consciousness, as a boundless experience to be seized upon immediately and enjoyed, rather than a new province still to be conquered. The world of poverty and policy, of humanism and humour, faded into insignificance before man's wonder at the forces of nature and the ecstasy of his liberated egotism. Everywhere we see a rejection of fact and method in the pursuit of a transcendent idea and of that Liberty which Ruskin in the prudence of later experience named a " treacherous phantom." This generous avidity of aspiration, outrunning reason instead of carrying it along with it, was the error at the outset which was certain to vitiate practice. Only slowly could men graduate in this new and vast school of life, and meanwhile in their hasty reaction from narrow criticism to extravagant sensationalism, they assured without knowing it the cosy mind and the cosy furniture of the mid-Victorian age. Men wounded in their desires to know the universe fell back upon a parish; the early creative passion of youth degenerated into a possessive policy, a desire as it were to console nerves which had been over-taxed by clinging to something secure and small and tangible, or, as we cannot help feeling even in Browning's *Rabbi Ben Ezra*, by settling down sagely in the chair of middle age to enjoy the creature comforts alike of body and mind.

In a particular sense also Romanticism encouraged the cult of unreality for its own sake. For men, in their longing to escape rather than depose the tyranny of fact, indulged in fantastic dreams and abstract emotions, travelled in fancy over great distances of space and time, hoping thus to enjoy in safety the sensations of a vaguely beautiful and possibly criminal past. This cultivation of the un-usual, no less than that of the universal, eventually taught man to see impartially, freeing his mind from the burden of association, and endowing it, through familiarity with the extraordinary, with a spirit of toleration and enterprise. Romanticism eventually develops into naturalism, and encourages the scientific attitude, but only after men have tired of worshipping the eccentric for its own sake and have applied their new curiosity, no longer the enraptured prey of absurd fiction, to the actual life about them. But while Romanticism finally liberated human con-sciousness and enlarged man's conception of life and morality, the incautious excesses inherent in its origin not only persisted, when the first energy of the movement had failed, in many a weak and sentimental affectation, but also excited resistance in the less adventurous elements of life as much towards the truths as the heresies of revolutionary doctrine. Convention hardened to combat an irresponsible Liberty, the instinctive loosening of traditional doctrine by a few resulted in an instinctive tightening of conventional dogma by the many, who demanded security before freedom, and nice sentiments before true passion. Respectability was the inevitable reply of common sense to reckless sensibility, convention and pseudo-morality to extravagance and pseudo-romance. Yet this compromise, the fruit of what was false in Byron and even in Shelley, owed its origin in part to Godwin. Rousseau's doctrines were dangerous for exaggerating the virtues of naturalism, Godwin's for concealing selfish prejudice under the cloak of temperate reason, and for robbing life of its human value and enslaving it to a barren scheme of thought. Rousseau was misleading for his exaggeration in his early writings, if not in those of his maturity, of the virtue of naturalism, Godwin for a similar exaggeration of rationalism. The one was an emotional egotist, the other a mental; the one sentimentalised life, the other disregarded her in his dogmatic individualism. In justice to Rousseau it must be said that in the works of his riper manhood he eschewed the early sentimentalism which was so fatal in its influences, disclaiming his ingenious worship of the state of pre-social nature and seeking the reality of freedom within society. But so plausible is the allurement of falsehood that the hasty theorisings of immature genius are generally found to exercise a profounder influence over an age than the less spectacular wisdom of experience. In justice, likewise, to Godwin's philosophic anarchism we must admit that his intentions were of the noblest, and that in his later years he modified his theory of a vague and universal benevolence and urged on men a more practical and particular charity. But he never realised that the very artificial institutions and conventions which he attacked as responsible for all human evil, were themselves the creation of that human nature which he wished to liberate; were merely the expression in fixed forms of the forces of self-interest and lust, forces destined to be for long far more powerful and general and determining factors in human affairs than any abstract reason. Godwin's creed, being less spectacular than Rousseau's, developed more slowly; but by way of Bentham and Mill, in whom it found a sublimated expression beyond its deserts, and through Macaulay, who infused its spirit into his interpretation of both history and literature, it issued at last in the calculating commercial rationalism of the mid-century, combining with the lingering fatalism of *laissez-faire* in a doctrine which approaches dangerously near a sanctimonious inhumanity.

Carlyle, who, having stripped the world of its clothes, was driven in desperation to supply it with a conscript's uniform, stands by right at the head of the mid-Victorian period, as Meredith fitly concludes it. He is the father of that too large and vague and magnificent humanitarianism, which was fated after long struggle and many a false treaty to come to terms with realism. The conflict of faith with fact, which makes his writing so often an uncomfortable experience, was never so extreme or bitter in those who followed, although it was often more pathetic. Such men as Macaulay, Arnold, Tennyson, or Jowett, just because they were not so spiritually intrepid, evolved in their different ways a working agreement, or what Professor Elton calls a " temperate idealism." Ruskin was generally inspired enough to rise above the conflict; Tennyson shows it in his attempt to combine a Romantic impulse with a Classical form; Mill suffered in health and spirits for a time, but fled from it to logic, as the Pre-Raphaelites did to the cultivation of beauty and artistic craft for its own sake and their own pleasure; Clough reduced it to a tragi-comedy; Newman raised it to a level of dignity and grace, as his subtle mind and sensitive soul engaged in a struggle in which the distinction between truth and falsehood is apt to disappear. For like Renan he was a master of sentimental casuistry. Many we fancy must have echoed his words: " The year is worn out; spring, summer, autumn, each in turn, have brought their gifts and done their utmost; but they are over, and the end is come. All is past and gone, all has failed, all has sated. We are tired of the past; we would not have the seasons longer; and the austere weather which succeeds, though ungrateful to the body, is in tone with our feelings and acceptable. . . . Life passes, riches fly away, popularity is fickle, senses decay, the world changes, friends die. One alone is constant; One alone is true to us; One alone can be true; One alone can be all things to us; One alone can supply our needs." But of what nature that One was, a reality or a delusion, a miracle or a scientific hypothesis, an inspiration or a despair, few of Newman's contemporaries dare candidly question. Only for a time could traditional faith cool their fever, like a scarred rock casting a fickle shadow over a weary land. Thus did fear and disappointment lead men everywhere to withdraw from their attack upon the unknown, not stoically, but in agony or confusion of mind, the poet to his craft, the prophet to social conditions, the devout to a state of uncomfortable compromise or to the discipline and forgetfulness of Rome. It matters indeed little how we name the parties to the conflict, whether reason opposed to romance, realism to sentiment, science to faith or sense to sensibility— between these two attitudes of mind the age was torn; and while it was a healthy instinct which urged them to exclude neither absolutely, it was dishonesty and the weight of tradition which forbade them to combine them truly. One party pleaded for the mind, the other for the heart, but few for the bold union of the two, so that either their sentiment outstripped their thought, or their thought lacked the breadth and sympathy of true sentiment.

The modern malady which Myers later described as " that *welt-schmerz*—that impersonal and indefinable melancholy," was the direct offspring of an infinite egotistic desire, which, when refused the satisfaction of easy, credulous expression, returned perforce on itself in petulant resignation. We meet on all sides with men and women of moral elevation, of stern or mild disinterestedness, discovering or affecting to discover for themselves a personal tranquillity. Men not strong enough to dispense with hope were yet hopeless of arriving at conviction. For they were born into an acquisitive rather than a creative age, an age lacking the energy for true idealisation, but yet morally superior to materialism. The naturally religious shared " a profound modification of received beliefs," that bitter experience of high aims negatived by uncertainty of creed and wavering of conviction. Thinking men got no certain answer to the question whether there was a moral government of the world. The faith in human perfectibility, which had inspired the early years of the century, had faded away, and men had lost suddenly the comforting assurance of a controlling providence, and were cast on their own resources. It is this which explains the intense moral sensitiveness of the time, unrelieved by positive action, and which led at last to the recurring cry, consciously enshrined in the positivists' creed, that men should order their own house aright and look for no external help or reward, nor any longer abandon themselves to a life principle, of which the virtue was now held in grave doubt.

The development of pure science only exaggerated the malady which it was finally to cure. For scientific materialism, not as Darwin stated it, but as the lay mind interpreted it, assumed a dogmatism no less assured than the religious, and dangerous than the hastily idealistic. A deification of fact was added to the prevalent indulgence of fancy, the proofs of natural selection adduced by Darwin were by many of his ignorant disciples applied mechanically to man. They supplied the terrible but rational explanation of that divine providence which such men as Dr. Arnold honoured with so remarkable a confidence, and thus, alongside the gospel of the Will of God, by which many justified alike the French Revolution, the Anglican Church, sweated labour and the deserving poor, arose the gospel of science, which gave to the utilitarian school an example in the laws of nature, not only for allowing the industrial machine to grind unimpeded on its ruthless way, but even for assisting it to do so more efficiently. The apparent fatalism of science and the fatal superstition of religion united to reduce men to impotence. It was only gradually that such men as Huxley and Wallace, who were more than pure scientists, having led men to appreciate the indifference and immorality and consistency of the cosmos, boldly stated that they were within limits masters of and not cogs in the machine. Nevertheless, although science tended to dehumanise men for a time, it cauterised the false sentiment of the age together with the true, and proved eventually a health-giving tonic. It invaded with its spirit and its method philosophy, sociology and history. Stubbs and Freeman succeed Macaulay and Froude, and in place of Carlyle's polemics we find Spencer quietly foreseeing the day when no man shall ask why he need help his neighbour. It affected pure literature more slowly, because poets were pursuing beauty with their eyes half-closed to life, and because science in material blindness tended to disregard the truth which resides most vitally in beauty.

In art and criticism, therefore, no less than in religion and economic thought, the results are clear. After Shelley's death, the idealistic wave, of which he was the crest, subsided, and the mid-Victorian poets lay in the trough of it, disturbed by Romantic cravings, which they tried to satisfy with safety and only succeeded in conventionalising. They lost

R

hope through hoping too much, for when they ceased from irrational effort, they ceased from rational too, and as the religious returned to a conventional God, so the poet turned to beauty, each seeking for comfort rather than vital experience,— a policy which left them puzzled and a little ashamed. The result was that no age was so incurably and bewilderingly romantic, while remaining polite, narrow and serious in its demeanour; no age hungered for the eternal with such inability to escape the boundaries of time, or showed more accumulative energy, and created so little that is permanent by virtue of its sincerity and strength. In each of the greater poets we detect a desire to produce something great in bulk rather than intense in spirit, if only to satisfy Macaulay's definition of those who " have ornamented the world." There is something pathetic in the spectacle of an age which more than any other accepted temporary and secondary values, aspiring to settle the problems of life for good and all, whether it be Spencer in his *Synthetic Philosophy*, or Mill in his search for " fixed and invariable laws," or Ruskin in his attempt to evolve an absolute æsthetic, or Tennyson to poetise a complete code of conduct. Men, still influenced by the assured impulse of Romanticism, could not realise that the world of human consciousness had become too complex to dismiss under simple and majestic formulas, or that there were many problematic things in life

about which they had every right to withhold an
opinion. The very fluency of their writing suggests
the tireless energy of the machines which were
multiplying about them, an energy inexhaustible
because facile, because they tended to move upon
the surface plane of life, and to avoid the ruts and
morasses where resistance would be met. But this
imperfect attempt to materialise universal ideas
without transgressing existing creeds and conditions,
to subdue a spiritual world to a system of thought
and manners, instead of to cultivate a right and
independent attitude of mind, could only end in
the creation of baffled aspirants like Sordello or
pathetic stoics like Empedocles. At the same time
it resulted in the emphasis of the form of art at the
expense of the spirit, of conscientious workmanship
independently of the idea which good craftsmanship
was meant to serve. The manner became grand
because the matter was small. " You are yet too
young to comprehend how much in life depends
upon manner," wrote Disraeli, and perhaps in an
age which failed so signally when it tried to produce
an art of ideas or discover true passion, such a
sentence spelt hope. Yet *In Memoriam* or *The Two
Voices* or even *Maud* dissatisfy us in spite of their
manner. Tennyson accepted life and thought as
it was conditioned by his time, but art must go
to uncultivated life, and wrestle with its crude
primary forces, and with those " great elementary

feelings " of which Pater spoke, but from which he withdrew rather fastidiously himself. When later in this period we come upon such true originals as the Brontë sisters, we discover what so few early Victorians knew,—the reality of the awful struggle for existence inevitable to both nature and man, a struggle which both life and science advertised, but which Victorian literature so slowly admitted, preferring quiet moralising or scrupulous handiwork at some distance from the crude human arena. This separation from reality—a logical consequence of the confusion of idealism, egotism and naturalism at the beginning of the century—was, we cannot doubt, the essential cause of the Victorian malady.

Even such men as Ruskin hated industrial ugliness more because it offended their private sense of beauty than for the agony of human waste which it implied, and when they greatly sympathised, it was without an intimate knowledge, and their reform suggestions were often more violent than considered, just as in their own art descriptive eloquence so often outsped observance. And as earlier the cult of power proved stronger than reason, so beauty came to be cherished as a sensation sufficient unto itself. Beauty was much coveted, much discussed and much acclaimed in the days when the *Germ* was first published, but man's fidelity to the lamp of beauty was more consistent than their service at the shrine of truth. It is for

this reason alone that so many of the flowers which
they cultivated in her honour have failed to withstand the " winter of our discontent "!   Those
strange sad faces which look out on us from the
canvasses of Rossetti or the pages of Pater,—what
are they but images of their creators' desire tan-
talised to the point of suffocation, emblems of the
time with its " sick hurry and divided aim "?
Poets and artists invented a type of beauty, as
moralists a code of conduct, and tried to perpetuate
their personal formulas by repetition, in place of
images drawn from life, ever renewing themselves
under different forms, while retaining an identity
of principle.   And because they were unable to find
truth in the life of their own time or in their own
emotions, many were driven to busy themselves
with the manners or the speech of the past.   But
their interest was often little more than a con-
noisseur's, and when they sought to renew in fact
either the Gothic or the Ballad or the Saga, they
generally lacked the vital and original impulse which
had once given, and might again give, reality to
these forms.   What was vivid and literal realism
to a poet or artist of the Middle Ages, whether it
was a Madonna or a Beatrice, was too often
only an industrious, if charming affectation to the
informed minds of the nineteenth century,—an
affectation which enabled them to escape from an
offensive actuality into a world of elegance and

grace, a world in which their senses might find respite and consolation.

2

It is indeed by examining the conflict of mediæ-valism and modernism that the triumphs and failures of the Pre-Raphaelite movement in poetry can be best assessed. One poet only, we think, will emerge from such an examination altogether successfully, and he is Rossetti. "Rossetti's figures," Lafcadio Hearn has written, "whether of the Middle Ages or of modern times, seem like the results of a double consciousness. We can touch them and feel them, although they are ghosts." It is in this true mastery of illusion that Rossetti's unique distinction lies. He perhaps alone of his day harmonised that conflict of opposites into which life had temporarily dis-integrated, that dualism between sensuality and spirituality, fancy and imagination, which revealed itself in a confusion of mediævalism and modernity, romance and realism. Thereby, as a poet at least, he escaped for the most part both the morbidity and affectation, which is so marked a feature of others of his school. Rossetti's poetry is, in short, symbolic and not allegorical; it achieves imaginative unity and reality; it embodies, despite its conscious manner, a new creative experience. It avoids alike the decorative and the neurotic. Possibly because of his Italian origin he succeeded in transcending, to a degree even beyond Browning, that movement which elsewhere shows itself as a spasmodic revolt against the tameness of mid-Victorianism and towards a more conscious self-analysis. Thus he did not take refuge from his time in an antique and artificial manner, but, while resorting to the past for its simpler manifestations of the beauty and anger of life, he concentrated also on it the subtleties of a modern consciousness, which had peered wonderingly into the dark places of the soul. Similarly he gave (notably in *The House of Life*) an organic form and a spiritual interpretation to that analysis of the physical which his age compelled. The singular magnitude of his achievement lay, then, in his uniting of the opposed elements of old and new in a fresh synthesis. This harmony of body and soul, this sincere revitalising of old forms, is rarely found in Morris, after his first unique volume, and save in part of *Sigurd*, where he quite miraculously loses himself in another age. It is rarer still in the work of Swinburne, who, for want of it, became the slave of fierce nostalgias and brilliant virtuosities, lacking for the most part coherent imagination. The general desire which inspired the movement to rescue pure æsthetic truth from the toils of convention commands our sympathy and admiration. But the Pre-Raphaelites as a whole quite failed to measure the subtleties of the problem which faces a modern poet, assuming from whatever motives a legendary theme, and they were too ready to confuse the beauty of art with a vague, charming romance. The modern poet must either by an act of pure imagination difficult to conceive reincarnate the past as it was, or he must endow it with his own heightened human consciousness. To exploit it merely for effects of superficial and arbitrary quaintness or to manufacture out of it, as Morris often did, an old-world tapestry, may prove a pleasant pastime, but it is to sacrifice originality to imitation, the soul of art to the body.

This cultivating of decoration for its own sake, and confusing of a narcotic twilight and a tropical excess with the exquisite daylight of true mysticism and the heightened speech of passion, is a marked feature of the whole movement. And such æsthetic insincerity is very prevalent throughout the whole Victorian age.

Tennyson himself essayed to write poems of simple life in the manner of Wordsworth, without walking the country lanes as his master did in humility of spirit. Others developed the mysterious in lieu of the mystical or the false eccentric, because they feared to study nature's own abnormality, or the slackly sentimental for lack of passion. This habit of cultivating things which were easy to control and of neglecting or discrediting the physical basis of life led to a moral and æsthetic provincialism, which not even Arnold's desire to " see things as they

really are " could altogether escape. The liberal
impulse which enabled him to pass beyond a local
and domestic view of English art and admit Europe
to his counsels, did not free him from social and
ethical bondage when he discussed its qualities;
rather he tended to legalise, by the grave dignity
of his utterance, a creed of culture which would tie
the imagination, eager for dangerous journeying, to
a professional guide, and end its passionate quests
in the continent of life for ever. But the higher life,
when it ceases to be perilous and to call upon all the
energies from moment to moment, degenerates surely
into a mere manner of living without offence to
educated sensibilities, and into the accumulation of
poetry over which, in Sir Henry Taylor's words,
" the passionate reason of man does not preside in
all its strength as well as in all its ardours." The
urbanity of " sweetness and light " approaches at
times the smug complacence of suburban manners,
the pathos of *Requiescat* draws as many false tears
to our eyes as true. And just as " conduct " was
preached as a dogma, instead of as the practical
expression of a continuous revelation, so poetry was
proclaimed as a criticism not of all the glory and
baseness of life, but of the life of the refined respect-
able man, whose sense of propriety was so sorely
tried by latent desires which he would not admit.
Beauty became one of the consolations of culture
in a crude world, a source of transient self-satis-

faction to those who could not relate themselves to
the eternal. Wordsworth had for Arnold " a healing
power," and Keble discussed poetry as a curative
medicine for the diseases of the soul. The age had
denied the life which it could not direct, and life
revenged itself. Men pleaded for medicine because
their bodies prospered and their souls were sick.
They longed for happiness, but they mistrusted
liberty, crying with less justice than Madame Roland:
" Liberty, liberty, what things are done in thy
name." And so only such a recluse as Emily Brontë
could find " in the bleak solitude many and dear
delights, and not the least and best beloved was—
liberty." The majority lacking liberty of soul clung
to security, vainly seeking to soothe their angry
nerves with the material solaces of society, and to
satisfy their starved senses with the luxuries or
castigate them with the precepts of art. Whigs
like Macaulay, and radical preachers like Ruskin
and Morris had a taste for feudal or mediæval conditions, largely because they seemed to guarantee a
safe, settled and courteous life (if only for the few),
and to stand firm and permanent against the threat
of catastrophe. But beneath their earnest cheerfulness, there lurked ever more insistently " doubt,
hesitation and pain," just as behind their drawing-
room courtesy the spectre of sweated industry
glided hungrily, discomfiting their sweetest sentiments and mocking their sublimest sermons. " We

have had enough of weariness, and dreariness, and
listlessness, and sorrow and remorse. We have
had enough of this troublesome world," wrote one
of them, but the truth was that they had not had
enough, that they could not escape from themselves
and the unreal life which their egotism, conspiring
with events, had constructed. The natural and the
supernatural were lost to them. God himself was
become more of a formula than a faith, an external
intelligence or a mechanical despotism, with which
they might not interfere, and they were lonely and
desperately self-conscious. Tennyson's frantic assertion, " You never, never can convince me that the
I is not an Eternal Reality," must have been echoed
in many a heart, or Browning's

> What is it that I hunger for but God?
> My God, my God, let me for once look on Thee,
> As though none else existed, we alone!

Amid all their apparent sociability, there lingers
this sense of a great and empty solitude, dim and
disillusioned; of an unhealthy silence, in which people
go on perpetually talking to ease the idle distraction
of their minds. For no one is so pitiable or so personal
as he who yearns for an impossible heaven without
the valiancy to struggle for it, at the possible cost
of self-respect, in the dark. This was the cause
of the self-consciousness, which Mill called " that
dæmon of the men of genius of our time, and to which
this age owes so much, both of its cheerful and its

energy, which yet serves a true and not distorted imagination, and which is therefore rational at its core. Prejudice and partisanship of their nature excite passion and so beget the matter of poetry. Reason tends to neutralise passion, unless it can be persuaded to serve and sublimate it into pure vision as in all the greatest moments of poetry (beyond the habitual reach of a Byron or a Swinburne) it has done.

Poets, however, looking back upon the last century, are with reason suspicious of prolific energies. They doubt the quality and the consequences of large emotions. For the leading figures of the Romantic revival threw off the control of tradition, whether embodied in an outworn moral or social code or in a cult of dead humanism, because they demanded the right to express their natures to the full. Ideally this should have led to a great imaginative revival and a restoration of absolute values to both life and art. In a few poets of genius and for a few brief years such an ideal was enthusiastically embraced, if often imperfectly realised. Ceasing merely to rebel rhetorically against relative standards, they visioned a life of true spiritual liberty. On a wave of emotional desire they mounted to a conception of absolute beauty and justice as imaginative as it was in the last resort sincerely humanitarian.

But a sensation, however high, of Paradise regained is a dangerous thing. Even the leaders of this movement frequently confused their facts and their ideals, mournful wisdom." Fear, shame and doubt are the offspring of this detached attitude of mind: they haunt the Victorian stage, like the witches in *Macbeth*.

And as with the century's advance men of true and honest genius sprang up, men virile and human, anxious and well-equipped, like Dickens and Reade and Kingsley, for warfare on all things mean and false, although powerful enough to triumph over the affectation of their times, they could not altogether escape its contagion. They were compelled to fight for their health against a creeping paralysis, and their work bears traces of the disease which they conquered. The strident tones of Carlyle recur again after the suave mid-season of unhealthy weather. Dickens has a false eccentricity as well as a true, a nerveless pathos and a noble pity, mincing sentiment and vast humanity. Strong men in their thirst for the genuine and the artless became at times clumsy, melodramatic, or hysterical. Force for force's sake exists alongside art for art's, a creature optimism balances a dilapidated pessimism. George Eliot has often the moral violence of an irritated governess, Browning that of an exasperated school-boy. Thackeray could not altogether escape the snobbery which he wrote a book to exterminate; two moral fairies haunted disastrously the kind heart of Kingsley; so normal a man as Browning in his revolt from stagnation and his inability to comprehend values was driven to express his health through pathology and to mingle in a confused creed logic, psychology and animalism. In Swinburne, however, all the vague sentiments of the age,—its paganism, mediævalism, radicalism and anticlericalism—became exaggerated gestures. Yet to the call for vigour and sincerity of impulse he sacrificed the duty of thought. And the lesson of reason and reality was not completely learnt by any Victorian novelist or poet until Meredith, while even in him the marriage of science and sense is not perfectly consummated.

The wit with which Meredith attacked false sentiment and its " fine shades " was often tainted with the spasmodic insincerity, the meretriciousness, of its victim, but it was sweetened too by a runaway humour unheard in English literature for many years. Morris was strong enough constantly to play the dilettante in poetry without prejudice to his powers, but Meredith was strong enough to play the clown! And in him, despite his occasional blatancy and distorted egotism, we enjoy again " glad confident morning." He is unashamed in body and in mind, crude sometimes, histrionic and overconscious, but valiant enough to admit the limitations of human knowledge, to endure with tranquillity the darkness, and glory in the imaginable splendour of the unknown. In his writing we discover no more the whine of doubt, the blush of shame, or the tactics of fear. The natural world, analysed by science, is sublimated by his mind, and rendered human and habitable by his instinct. He knows that a thoughtless naturalism will not suffice, but he does not, as Wordsworth seems sometimes to do, sacrifice half his joy in life to the discovery, and so his morality is vital and impassioned as well as wise and true. Perhaps the philosophy upon which that morality is reared is best summarised in the attitude of his hero Redworth to the incomparable Diana:

> She gave him comprehension of the meaning of love; a word in many mouths, not often explained. With her, wound in his idea of her, he perceived it to signify a new start in our existence, a finer shoot of the tree stoutly planted in good gross earth; the senses running their live sap, and the minds companioned and the spirits made one by the whole-natured conjunction. In sooth, a happy prospect for the sons and daughters of Earth, divinely indicating more than happiness, the speeding of us, compact of what we are, between the ascetic rocks and the sensual whirlpools to the creation of certain nobler races, now very dimly imagined.

Or more passionately and intimately in *A Faith on Trial*:

> Rejoice we to know not shame,
> Not a dread, not a doubt; to have done
> With the tortures of thought in the throes,
> Our animal tangle, and grass
> Very sap of the vital in this:
> That from flesh with spirit man grows
> Even here on the sod under sun.

Meredith is perhaps the first of the moderns, because in him body and mind and soul are one; reason is become a passion, and passion an art. English literature had passed through the high and hasty aspiration of revolutionary dogma, and a period of clouded complexity, in which the discoveries of natural science, though limited to fact, were the only complete achievement, to renew its strength in the physical and philosophic candour of creative evolution.

Reason, to use Professor Elton's phrase, had now caught up the facts which aspiration had ignored. " Science so enlarged and harmonised " as Swinburne wrote, " gives me a sense as much of rest as of light "; and where Dickens was too greatly charitable himself to recognise the full savagery of necessity and the unkindness of the world, and where Browning overleapt indiscreet calamity in his insistent demand for a happy, comfortable futurity, and his staking of everything on the non-existence of absolute evil, Meredith found in the life of man as in the processes of nature an evolutionary struggle through error and defeat to knowledge of self and of truth, a struggle which gave zest to joy, and point to pain, and in which there was no security save in unguarded effort, and no liberty without the recognition of a callous external law, a struggle in which the race went not to the timidly pious or the correctly moral, but to the physically fearless and the spiritually strong. Thus after half a century of doubt and disenchantment, of secret dissent and outward conformity, the spirit of Shelley's Titan re-discovered itself in English literature, enriched and stabilised, inviting men once more to be " good, great and joyous, beautiful and free."

CHAPTER IX

THE MODERN SPIRIT

The world has tried fighting, and preaching and fasting and buying and selling, pomp and parsimony, pride and humiliation—every possible manner of existence in which it could conjecture there was any happiness or dignity: and all the while, as it bought, sold, and fought and fasted and wearied itself with policies and ambitions and self-denials, God had placed its real happiness in the keeping of the little mosses of the wayside and of the clouds of the firmament. Now and then a wearied king, or a tormented slave, found out where the true kingdoms of the world were, and possessed himself in a furrow or two of garden ground, of a truly infinite dominion.

JOHN RUSKIN, *Hopes and Fears for Art.*

I

OUR age, we are often told, is predominantly scientific. The fact implies both danger and hope. For if science can more and more teach men the need of intellectual honesty, it can also starve their sympathies. It is not generally recognised that the mind alone is as material as the body alone. The sins of the old world against the Holy Ghost were customarily sins of the flesh, surrenders to lust; those of the modern world are more often sins of the mind, surrenders to logic. For the spirit can be killed either by lust or logic, or, worst of all, by both in combination. On the other hand it is upon physical force and logical faculty rightly blended that the soul depends for energy and direction. The mechanical intelligence which science uses to examine facts is in itself both limited and unmoral. It will apply itself to the discovery of poison gas with as earnest an efficiency as to that of a cure for cancer. Alone it is an exact instrument for calculating cause and effect within a given circle of particulars. In the integrity of its method it offers an example well worth emulating by vague and careless minds, but only when its impartial equity is directed towards life as a whole, and when an appreciation of the beautiful is added to a demand for the precise, do science and art unite to form both a religion and a morality, to satisfy man's longing for vital perfection, and his enquiry after the data upon which he should base his actions. In the poetry of to-day we see the first sign on a wide scale of this combination of accurate thought and sympathy. All evolution in art as in life is towards a higher, more intense and more embracing form of consciousness. This is the only true aristocracy, and the danger of the scientific spirit is that it tends to the accumulation of knowledge instead of the comprehension of values. Modern poets in their fear of sentimentalism and in their fidelity to facts have for the most part at present an incomplete grasp of idealism, a diffidence sometimes bordering upon scepticism. They dare not devote their sensibility to life for fear of error or excess, because in the poetry

s

of the last age they see so often examples of an emotional conviction imposed arbitrarily upon facts which, rightly considered, denied it. They see, in short, truth sacrificed to feeling. They are timid, therefore, of attempting to comprehend the cosmos, and some of them exaggerate their own egotism, and thus dwarf their sensibility in their consciousness of the rights and responsibility of the human will. They are in a less aggravated way like some of Dostoievsky's characters who compel themselves to do things against which their whole natures revolt, that they may at least be sure of their own human prerogative; who are even in the last degree prepared to kill themselves to assert their own wills. Yet already it is tentatively recognised that an assertion of will, no more than an indulgence of appetite or a barren intellectuality can bring man happiness or reconcile his aspirations with his environment, but that only through imaginative effort, that is through the light of reason working in harmony with, but also more finely than the forces of nature, can men learn the truth of life and how to realise through it the highest possibilities of their humanity.

This fusion of all the human faculties is still to be realised in the future; in preceding chapters we have traced briefly how in man's nature a state of dualism sprang up with developing consciousness out of an instinctive unity. We can only vision by faith the possibility of a new and ultimate reconciliation. At present man's body made half-conscious of mind, has lost the secret or the desire of mere physical satisfaction, while his mind, uncertain how to form a free but wise alliance with the body, seeks in vain for intellectual certainty; and so he is content merely to protest against a supposed celestial providence, long accepted blindly by simple minds —but now discredited. This revolt against the sanctifying of nature is perhaps the most marked and hopeful symptom of the modern consciousness.

It is the latest tendency of Protestantism, the culmination of the doctrine of free-will, the consummation of humanity; and when the critical element in it has ceased to preponderate in its denial of life, and men are content rather to welcome all experience positively, and are able to discriminate the true from the false in the very act of accepting, Protestantism will have ceased to be a partial instrument of progress and a negative check upon natural impulse, and will finally justify itself in the complete realisation of human as distinct from animal values.

At present the critical attitude, of which circumstances have, particularly during the last hundred years, enforced the need, exists to a degree prejudicial to great creative energy. For manifestly it must always be the hardest of all tasks to write great poetry—poetry of compelling power and subtle rhythm, of daring image and dithyrambic

and because their impulse was fundamentally naturalistic, moral and æsthetic anarchy soon appeared. Men had the will to cast off artificial restraints, but they lacked the power to direct their liberated energies towards a comprehended ideal. Such a one as Byron, for instance, sentimentalised his sensations and called it a philosophy, and justified licence by deifying the human will. Men were too naturalistic to criticise nature and too impatient to study humanity, and so their idealism quickly degenerated for want of humble insight and the support of first principles. An individualism which originally justified itself by being cosmic became even inhuman when it was merely selfish.

An age of elegant but indolent compromise followed: romantic sensationalism was turned to the uses of pleasure, and creative values forgotten in the placid decoration of an acceptable existence. Ethical effort disappeared in material satisfaction. Social platitudes took the place of ardent humanitarianism, extreme respectability that of instinctive licence. Upon this unhealthy calm Science advanced like a surgeon, but was mistaken for a bandit. The earlier romantic movement failed because human intelligence was then unequal to the strain of emotional freedom; the discomfort of the middle period was due to the fact that true mental honesty came when only tenacious sentiments survived. We see it in the religious anguish of such as Clough,

and from the doubt and diffidence of that time
two impulses emerge: an uncritical reaction to
realism, a worship of fact as fact on the principle of
science, and, in opposition, a further refining of
false or secondhand sentiments and an attempt
to conceal the lack of creative idealism behind
technical perfection.

2

This confusion of values, this vacillation between
a complacent optimism and a cruel pessimism, has
persisted almost to our own day. We may illustrate
the reaction to naturalism or realism and the
consequent sacrifice of intellectual and so of moral
values, by a brief reference to three significant
personalities—those of Emerson, Whitman and
Nietzsche. Emerson is still akin to the earlier
Romantics in his genial optimism and his enthusiastic and vague humanity; Whitman's is the
undiscriminating voice of democracy, which far
from transcending distinctions, is vulgarly oblivious
of them; Nietzsche is the prophet of that violent
exultant pessimism, of which the Great War was in
some ways the ghastly expression. Each was a poet
in his kind, each was the servant of an unexamined
ecstasy, and a rebel against the tameness and the
cumulative lethargy of their times. Each failed to
reconcile what is at heart an animal arrogance

with the lessons of experience. Revolt was indeed justified, but it was vitiated in them by the direction they took and the methods they championed.

Emerson's creed is the least misleading, because he was by temperament mild, and beneath his transcendental enthusiasms cherished a fastidious soul. His essay on *Nature* is perhaps the best manifesto of his faith and is also nearer constructive argument than anything which he wrote. Here the fervid prophet of happiness and hope, the appealing figure of impassioned exhortation and benevolent mysticism, tries to explain his faith in life, and justify his love of it. Of his rare singleness of aim we can entertain no doubt. Always he exhorted men " to seek truth and ensue it "; but in his very impassioned utterance there was a fatal flaw. In discrediting the penny-wisdom of pedantry, in denouncing the cowardice of that calculating intelligence, which seemed to be dwarfing the stature of his times, he denied also the rights of reason. He champions what he conceives to be the highest faculties at the expense of everything else, and thus he sacrifices the one criterion by which we can distinguish idealism from sentimentalism. This is the root of our dissatisfaction with Emerson. He does not check his observance; he scorns observance. Nature to him is an appendix of the soul, life an ineffable essence pervading and dissolving matter. He is in too ecstatic a sympathy with the spirit to cast his eye disinterestedly over the body. We can accept his assurance of the essential spirituality of things; we can sympathise with his preference for creative intelligence or imagination to the "wintry light of understanding." So long as he remains on this high ground he can flood the soul with light. But in doing so he either leaves the world with high disdain in darkness or casts upon it a spurious sunlight, solacing himself with the assurance that all disagreeable appearances will quickly vanish from the scholar "reading God directly." But this is surely a doctrine of mystical indifference, of entranced self-absorption, which no Western intelligence can accept. It is emotionalism arming itself with sanctity against the cruel neutrality of fact, an airy sublimation in fact of the pioneering spirit of his fathers, who had no wish or time for thought, who were compelled to press on in blind optimism, because only so could they subdue a hostile material world. And in its pale transcendentalism, remote from practical affairs, it commended itself greatly to a business community, who wished to indulge in high sentiments, without putting them into practice. Certainly the essence of Emerson's message is an eternal one. It is that we should put ourselves diligently into harmony with the creative forces of life; thus shall we realise beauty, goodness and truth. It is his only theme, but about it his enthusiasm raised a pile, not of argument but of rhapsody. In

this compelling unity he merged all distinctions,
and when he tried to relate his theme to actual life,
he had not the courage to look her in the face. One
of his orations, for example, is entitled *The Method
of Nature*; but if we look for any new light to
be cast upon the ancient dualism between man and
necessity, reason and the brute forces of the world,
beauty and truth, we shall be grievously disappointed.
Emerson sees nature only in her supernatural
significance, he worships only her genius and blindly
credits her with his own morality. His " laws of
nature " are simply another term for the old benevolent providence of God. Nature was to him full of
rich conveniences, and he sank contentedly into her
luxurious upholstery without questioning her manner
of life. So seeing only "the mystery of nature happily
displayed," he could say that all things were moral
and that nature was ever the ally of religion—a truth
which needs very clear definition, if it is not to
become a pitfall of error. But definition can only
come through the intellect, and this Emerson, in
his exhortation " to cherish the soul," was only too
prone to slight. To be an evangel of the eternities
and scorn the wisdom of the ages is a popular but
short-sighted programme. Emerson did not realise
that the only way to ensure sincerity, and to avoid
the warping of literature not only by custom,
but also by valueless emotion, was by a sympathetic development of the reason. Virtue can only

face the darkness and survive if it be the fine flower of thought.

These sentimental and anarchic tendencies, this rejection of critical values, we find exaggerated and already showing destructive symptoms in the more vigorous but less sensitive genius of Whitman. In the best of his verse his instinctive energy, breaking through all restraints, sweeps us along with it. He exhilarates us mightily like a March wind. We are content to forget his unconsidering superficiality; we surrender to his strong naturalism as to a cleanly sensation, and go back to a life of care refreshed. But short of his pure abandonment, when becoming an impersonal voice of life, he realised the disinterestedness of the sun shining alike on the just and the unjust, the rhetorical journalism, which his less inspired verse represents, troubles us with commonplace chaos without freeing us, and we resent his confused barbarism. Whitman was a robust American Rousseau. For all his boast of being in the van of progress, the poet of reality and hope, he represents a throw-back to the past as surely as Goethe does a break-through to the future. It is significant that the doctor who attended him considered him " the most *natural* man I have ever met." He described himself as the poet of body and soul; and it is true that in him is found that physical mysticism which asserts a quality of spirituality, through disregarding all thought and giving ideal expression to an animal well-being. But such spirituality has to be translated into human terms before it becomes either a pure or a practical ideal and ceases to be merely an invigorating sensation. The history of civilisation, which Whitman so grandly disregarded and often so pettily derided, reveals the halting process of that transmutation. Whitman, however, in his scorn of artistic cant and of greedy caution neglected even more flagrantly than Emerson the wisdom of artistic courtesy and the necessity of rational endeavour. The undeveloped conditions under which he lived amid young and sparse institutions encouraged him to believe that a new civilisation could be built up, free from the errors of the old, on a basis of the more agreeable manners of savagery. We can still learn much from the virtues of the savage, if only we are sufficiently alive to his vices. But this Whitman never was. The irregular manner in which his unselected impressions of life, from which he had derived no philosophy, expressed themselves, was typical of his whole view of life, which was blind to the laws of evolution and responded ardently to nature's creative energy and impartiality, but little to her formative discretion. The chaos of his poems, at their best in elemental rhythm and sweeping resonance, at their worst in irregular and uncritical accumulation, was typical also of his view of that young democracy, " radical, true, far-scoped, and thorough-going," which was to teach the world a new robust hygiene, and of which he, in his transcendental egotism, his arrogance, gracelessness, and sincerity, was the incarnation. For his idea of democracy, when he failed to sublimate it into such a phrase as " I think the soul will never stop or attain to any growth beyond which it shall not go," was as insolent as any tyranny, and in his attack on every other kind of society other than democracy, he failed to distinguish between the idea for which royalty or aristocracy stood, that of service, responsibility, and grace, and the mere abuses which attached to their failure in fact. But naturalism cannot distinguish the idea and the fact, and Whitman was animal even in the serenity which he desired. He craved that freedom from nervous strain which is an inevitable part of mental effort. He contrasted man with the animals to his grave discredit, but he did not realise that animals are " so placid and self-contained " just because they are irresponsible, that humanity is a privilege and a distinction, which has to be paid for. He lacked, in short, any fine perception of the values which separate the great and the rare from the worthy but mediocre. His love of the wholesome average, of " the throbbings of the great heart of humanity itself," blinded him to the higher intensities of emotion and the subtler values of thought which democracy itself must cultivate if it is not to remain as vulgar and narrow in its ignorance as so-called aristocracy has so often proved in its learning.

Finally, in Nietzsche we see a rebel against sluggish convention and against a facile and at times cruel optimism, definitely championing an ideal of destruction. In Schopenhauer, to whom Nietzsche for all his later denunciation owed much, the denial of the life-force was gentle and mournful, fastidious too as was the temper of his mind. In his successor it was exultant. The creative energy of the nineteenth century having either soared away from actuality into abstract metaphysics or, wearied by immature effort, subsided into sleepy sentimentalism, is by Nietzsche hysterically translated into a vital negative. Through all the writing of his maturity, particularly his *Zarathustra* and *Ecce Homo*, this worship of the destructive force of elemental nature as the only creative reality in a world stifled by sentimental convention, is apparent. Enraged by the religious and artistic nostalgia of his times, by their complacent optimism and their selfish possessiveness, Nietzsche embraced a conscious barbarism, and would have exchanged all the hardly-won perquisites of humanity, all the refinements of the ages, for the physical health which he and his generation craved. His distinction is that he was an honest realist, while his contemporaries were for the most part dishonest idealists. But a realist can only be true to fact; he cannot be true to truth.

And so Nietzsche proved as false in his open-eyed deification of nature's brutality as Emerson was in his sentimental blindness to it. Because human life had grown mean and somnolent, overburdened too with cumulative and unassimilated facts, he cried that man should score out his humanity, and become not only a destructive force, as Nature is, but an egotistic force also, which nature in her disinterested creativeness can never be. It seemed to him that only by radiantly denying his inheritance of beauty and sensibility, only by sinking back into the physical, and turning resolutely away from an insidious eternity, could man regain his health. And it was health which he sought rather than truth—in this so typical of all the great minds of the nineteenth century.

Thus he humiliated his eager intellect to serve natural values rather than to transmute them. He urged that man should realise life by denying it ruthlessly and asserting only himself; that with an ecstatic categorical negative he should reject the joy of true creativeness, because it had come to represent so generally an idle, parasitic and self-gratifying pleasure; that he should regain truth through pain, his own and the world's, and that instead of trying to realise life at its highest positive value through love, the essence of rational humanity, he should realise it through hate, that is, through the intellectual exploitation of brutality. Thus in

Nietzsche creative instinct turned upon itself. He preached intellectual barbarism as the antidote to spiritual hypochondria. In Rousseau and the Romantics creative naturalism had gone astray for want of rational direction, in Nietzsche and his disciples it is directed—but to Nihilism.

Nevertheless, even in this confusion of the positive spiritual values of humanity, with their degradation in the selfish culture which stifled the nineteenth century, and therefore in Nietzsche's dithyrambic denial of both, we can read the primitive expression of that spirit of dissection and analysis, by which the old elements of life have been disintegrated, and a new orientation assured. The hysterical negative has become in subtler minds a determination to study life and nature with critical caution. Moreover, in such writers as Dostoievsky the refusal of sentiment, so clamorous and egotistic in Nietzsche, appears as a creed of inspired self-negation, a feeling out towards a higher harmony for man, an attempt to prophecy, even through a pit of squalor, a new dispensation under which the physical and the spiritual will at last be reconciled in truth.

Meanwhile, in England and France at least, the last years of the century witnessed, in opposition to this crude return to Nature, an attempt by men of talent rather than of genius, not to purge sentiment, but to refine it by purely artistic means. The result was preciosity,—the cultivation of forms for their

own sake, of a beauty distinct indeed from the up-
holstered ugliness of the world against which its
creators rightly rebelled, but lacking the life and
substance which in the parallel movement existed
in an only too fatal and misdirected abundance.
Feeling an acute distaste for the externals of Victorian life, its satisfied Philistinism, its moral and
social hypocrisies, its sombre intolerance, its middle-
class greed, which everywhere stifled æsthetic significance, these men were driven to cultivate in self-
defence, not only an affected egotism, but a hot-house
art, divorced from life. Grace and singularity of
manner were championed in the face of conventional
ugliness. But the movement represented a change of
form rather than a change of spirit. The poetry
which was created as a challenge to indolent respectability was itself more of an exquisite idleness than
an exquisite activity. Its form was frequently that
of art, but in essence it was generally as empty,
luxurious and self-indulgent, as far from the strength
and joy of imaginative life as the suburban sloth and
middle-class formulas against which it rebelled. That
a quality of decadence was inevitable to all the finer
spirits of the last half-century was inevitable. For
decadence implies a failure on the part of man to
adapt himself to his environment, and the sickness
of soul, which such a divorce from the positive
forces of life involves. The world had denied beauty
and truth, and those who wished to realise these in

themselves could only do so by denying the pre-valent values of the world. But this neurosis, which must indeed be an inevitable accompaniment of all spiritual effort, until the normal values of life are bettered, can be either a germ of weakness latent in a positive assertion of values, or it can so infect and depress the spirit of the artist that his soul indeed falls sick, and his creative power deteriorates and finally wilts away. He has then neither the energy for violent discontent nor for that biting scepticism into which an artist's spiritual generosity has so often been converted by a complacent material world. He relapses into a faded cynicism, a fastidious pessimism, or that cult of exquisite, but jaded unreality, which was so prevalent in the poetry of the nineties.

3

There was, then, an inclination among men during the last half of the nineteenth century either to sacrifice their artistic conscience to a crude naturalism, or their spiritual life to their artistic conscience.

Zola chanting a hymn of praise to the undifferentiated forces of life, magniloquently entitled " Fécondité," "Vérité," and " Travail," may stand as the prototype of the one tendency, Flaubert toiling after " le mot juste," as that of the other. In this dilemma the century ended, and we may begin gradually to date the distinctive appearance of the modern spirit.

T

The task before the modern poet was to adopt the accurate observation of fact inherent in science, but to transcend its material limits by imaginative force and relate particular experiences to a universal conception. At his best, therefore, we find in him a consistent concentration on the intellectually real, a desire to see nature and man as they are, and honour them with all the resources of his understanding, rather than to feel vague personal emotions and spend all his intellectual powers in embellishing them. His accurate workmanship, his love of the pointed, vivid epithet, corresponds to his accurate observation; his humanitarianism may not advertise itself in large creeds, but it is true because based on fact. It shows itself in careful sympathy for all things, however humble, not in sentimental effusions that gratify the self. He may accept contemporary standards of morality no more than the Romantics: but he does so in no spirit of licence, but because he knows that general creeds must sacrifice truth to utility. The complexity of modern existence and the growth of particular observation have killed simple faiths and ambitious optimisms, and discredited for the poet such general catchwords as love, beauty or patriotism; the individual mind no more now surrenders to them than to the cosmos. It cultivates self-discipline, self-expression, and above all, self-responsibility. Its beliefs and passions must be tested on the anvil of actuality.

It will only approach the absolute through the relative, the universal through the particular; the human soul in all honesty ·stakes out claims against the universal.

Modern poetry at its best is the fruit of this accurate but unambitious insight. Inevitably it often falls short of this. It may remain a mere mental revolt from sentiment, in which the poet indulges his cleverness in conceits, or cynicisms, or frivolities; or his fear of self-delusion and his resolute concentration on fact may show itself in an unsympathetic hardness of expression, a brazen quality, fatal to music. Or, again, in his distrust of immediate attacks on the absolute, he may never escape from himself, but remain narrowly self-conscious, registering relative experiences personal to himself—a scientist not converted into a poet.

In his desire also to connect more truly the sensuous and the spiritual, and to insist upon their necessary inter-relationship, the modern writer is as apt to exaggerate the claims of the physical as the Victorians, though their neglect was to impoverish the spiritual. This tendency is clearly marked in the philosophy of Mr. D. H. Lawrence, who in his revolt from the cloying embrace of Victorian sentiment, with its exaggeration of the feminine virtues of sympathy, sensitiveness and pity, has fiercely championed the aggressive male virtues, claiming that only through the friction of physical conflict can the distinctive lines of personality be preserved. and life escape enervation. But for the achievement of art, rude material health is as inadequate as spiritual sickness; to divorce the real from the ideal as futile as to divorce the ideal from the real. The modern, in refusing a " foreground art," in trying to mirror that conflict between man's morality and nature's, and to record the interdependence of flesh and spirit, may relapse, as we have said, into a merely scientific reporting of the physical, in which the life of the senses is rarely keyed up to that pitch where spirit begins to be expressive.

Nevertheless it cannot but be good that men should be inoculated by reason against self-satisfaction and all sentimental formulas, that they should refuse to live any longer on the surface agreeably, pretending to a health and a morality which they do not feel, that they should dig down once more into actuality to build up idealism afresh.

We may admit that the building has scarce begun as yet, that most writers have been fully occupied dismantling the old edifice, and that there has been too much grovelling in the ruins. It is often with justice that moralists point the accusing finger, but often also with too little understanding of causes, and too weak a creative faith in the future. For it is possible to use sentimental disillusionment to quicken and not dull the spirit, to face facts without losing that sympathy for profuse nature, that emotional breadth of vision, which, if often abused, is yet the only passport to any intimate apprehension of life.

In English poetry at the moment it must be admitted that the reaction from vapid idealism or sentimental falsehood has encouraged in some quarters a cult of genial dullness, in others a decorative or realistic excess, and generally an avoidance of passion and thought, of significant selection or significant synthesis.

Of some modern poets we feel that they are sensitive, tolerant and talented; that they could turn out pleasant and finished verses to order on any concrete subject from a dog to a door-handle. They observe the small details of nature with a kindly curiosity, and report of her with a dainty daring. They lavish whimsies and faintly provocative emotions upon rather commonplace situations; but for the heightened speech of passion, touching the heart of things overmasteringly, we look almost in vain. So often an accomplished technique serves only a lethargy of soul, and the necessity imposed upon these poets of keeping us awake by crafty verbal surprises soon fails of its purpose. We weary of the coquetry of conceits, and, as with a building covered with nicely-trimmed ivy, we thirst for something bare and stark and strong.

In others, more daring and experimental both in form and content, we recognise sometimes miracles of virtuosity, striking achievements in the conscious manipulation of sounds and images, of words treated objectively like counters, or rather like hard splintered stones or shining jewels, but which, however, disappoint when judged as the mediums of human experience. In the very strained short-hand of their utterance we diagnose fever symptoms, the sign of tired nerves recording life at high pressure, with everywhere a sharp focus and an inability to apportion distances, rather than of sensibility absorbing experience, passion heightening it, and vision interpreting it through a scale of values. That such poets are discovering a new technique adequate to reflect the hurried impressionism, forced on men by the conditions of modern, mechanical city life, is certain. That such impressionism can discover for itself new methods of achieving unity and rhythm, other than the old, which are based on the spiritual and physical requirements of a less fevered pulse, is possible. But until such a unifying method is discovered, poetry of this order must remain incomplete and experimental. And it would even seem probable that modern impressionism, in its nervous unrest, is of its nature incapable of achieving any unity beyond that of the disconnected particular—is in fact engaged solely in shattering it. In so far of course as impressionism implies the denial of representation, the rejection of irrelevant detail, and the bold interpretation through actuality of personal values, it has been a necessary part of all great art. But in modern art the means has tended to become an end; a snatching at significant moments and details has very often displaced all attempt at relating a significant detail to a significant whole. The modern body may be tuned to a higher pitch, and so sensitive to new and subtler tones in the scale of life, but though experiences multiply, the laws of composition still remain. They may be the more difficult to apply, and call for readjustment and modification, but they are no less necessary, if art, as distinct from sensationalism, is to be achieved.

Finally, in other poets we meet with an indiscriminate surrender to those impressions, memories and desires, which float in the pool of the subconscious and rise to the surface fortuitously. These poets by good fortune may and do by this method apprehend and embody moments of pure and absolute reality. But for want of selection such convincing moments are overwhelmed in a mass of trivial irrelevance. Their flashes of imagination are like lightning in a bank of dreary cloud. The censorship of reason, as necessary in the discrimination of the subconscious as of the conscious, if æsthetic significance is to be attained, is here as unexercised in its power of rejection as in its construction of a sustained and unified vision of life. Of this also the want of homogeneous form in certain writers of free verse is a superficial symptom. Their weakness, no less than their strength, is that of the child. Doubtless in Classical Art, the laws of composition have often, as dogmas imposed from without, trespassed on life, or a too severe and conscious critical attitude has impoverished the matter of experience. On the other hand, in Romantic Art, that evocation of form, the materialisation as it were of the essence of things from within, has tended towards an uncritical and uncentralised profuseness.

Between these two extremes the great work of art lies. It combines form and chaos, binding the sense-perceptions, which provoke to ecstasy and invite the complete surrender of the artist's veto-power, into a pattern, dictated by controlling reason, a scheme which illuminates the tumult of life, by compelling it into harmony and unity.

Thus a true work of art should enclose us within itself, shutting us out from the actual world in its own unique domain. It should be like a dream of perfect completeness and symmetry rounded with a sleep, so far as the trivialities of life are concerned. It must therefore reveal no flaws in its structure or texture, through which our consciousness can stray out into the world of insignificant actuality—that exigent chaos, which life, unsubdued by the presiding genius of a great artist, must generally appear.

The weakness, however, of impressionism is that too often it lacks this organic self-sufficiency, this formal completeness.

4

But such imperfections do not discredit the modern spirit, they merely point its dangers, and although a desire to be critically positive and spiritually honest is, of course, not the peculiar perquisite of the younger generation, but has belonged to individuals in many epochs, we believe it never to have inspired so generally a collective group, not of artistic or intellectual giants, but of modest young men living in close touch with humble human affairs. That intellectual judgment should enter so generally into lyrical writing is indeed a new departure, uncontemplated by the Elizabethans who sang as birds, or the Augustans who wrote for clubs and drawing-rooms, or the Romantics who made instinctive melancholy melodious. Certainly one of the results is that the broad stream of natural rhythm is split up into innumerable eddies and ripples, and its fluidity at times congealed, because human sensibility is in the ascendant and is so much more differentiated than nature's, while poetry is less often a stream than a country, of which all the roads are " nerves of noble thought."

By contrasting Mr. Abercrombie's noble *Marriage Song* with Spenser's *Epithalamion* we can calculate our losses and our gains. The importance of the modern lyric is not so much its music as its sensitive apprehension of truth. And truth has a music of its own which resolves the discord of life. It is a balance between accurate observation and personal feeling. Sympathy is extended to the animal and vegetable worlds equally with the human, whether in Edward Thomas' interpretation of *Aspens* or Mr. Shanks' of the sea in *The Rock Pool*, or in Mr. Nichols' intimate farewell to a beloved spot:

> O bronzen pines, evening of gold and blue,
> Steep mellow slope, brimmed twilit pools below,
> Hushed trees, still vale dissolving in the dew,
> Farewell! Farewell! there is no more to do.
> We have been happy. Happy now I go.

And among animals truly imaged we have Julian Grenfell's *Greyhound*, Mr. Hodgson's *Bull*, Mr. Sturge Moore's *Gazelles* or, in a lighter but no less discriminating vein, Mr. Munro's *Cat*; while Mr. Freeman can give life and history to an inanimate chair. Nothing is too humble for their notice or too insignificant for their commiseration. Perhaps the most poignant of all such sensitive appreciation of the lot of humbler beings is Mr. James Stephen's *The Snare*, with its agonised pity for a trapped rabbit:

> And I cannot find the place
> Where his paw is in the snare!
> Little one! Oh! little one!
> I am searching everywhere.

Of a generous and selfless understanding of the pain and struggle in disregarded human lives there are many examples. We may mention Mr. Masefield's lines to his mother, Mr. Blunden's *Almswomen* and Wilfrid Owen's *Miners*. It is found with noble consistency in the work of Mr. Wilfrid Gibson.

Such poems may seem at first sight unambitious, but because they are readings of life, such as only a love inspired, but not confused by sentiment, could make, they are nearer to reality, and so to true beauty, than any selfishly cultivated loveliness. And from a level of particular consciousness they rise every now and then under the impulse of more urgent passion to a universal comprehension in which limited experiences are fused into that absolute identification with life which is beyond either pain or recrimination, as in Wilfrid Owen's *Strange Meeting*, or in Mr. Hodgson's glorious *Song of Honour*, where the conscious notes of human existence are lost at last in the elemental song.

> I heard it all, I heard the whole
> Harmonious hymn of being roll
> Up through the chapel of my soul. . . .

This modern spirit, which we may call poetical honesty, we taste constantly both in its richness and its insipidity in twentieth century verse. It is to be found of course in the work of all great poets, and nowhere more consistently than in the poetry of the Poet Laureate and Mr. Hardy, who, like all true genius, were in advance of their times, and both of whom, by different approaches, capture the Absolute. It were also foolish to argue that the spirit of Romanticism is

in any way discredited, because of a temporary reaction again those elements in the nineteenth century
movement, which have been proved false. True
liberty is not defamed by licence. Rather is its
essential truth confirmed by an understanding of
what was adulterated in men's first enthusiastic
conception of it. All that was vitally universal in
Shelley, in Hugo and in Goethe lives to-day even
more surely than the passionate naturalism of the
Elizabethans. For it is nearer to our human and
rational needs. Indeed, we may say that above the
small fluctuations of fashion we cannot henceforth
be ever again anything but romantic in spirit, and
demand the same infinite aspiration, the same faith
in evolutionary betterment, the same universal
humanity of our poets, as was voiced amid much
hasty error at the beginning of the last century.
Romanticism has enlarged man's consciousness for
good. We can never return to a poetry based upon
narrow and privileged sympathies. Only at present
we are above all anxious that our Romanticism
should be true; psychoanalysis, for example, is
simply Romanticism passing through a period of
self-examination.

In the best modern verse, therefore, we find much
that beside the irregular triumphs of transcendent
genius is tame, but little that is affected, deluded,
or insincere; we feel often the lack of urgent passion,
but we bless the absence of false sentiment. The

modern poet may sometimes stay on a material
plane for fear of falling into an emotional chasm,
and a general avoidance of extremes is noticeable
which deprives us as often of spiritual heights as
of sensual depths. For poets have ceased to believe
implicitly in the virtue of the life-principle, or the
easy perfectibility of man. Yet if they are too timid
to see nature in her whole magnificence, they
are too sane to make moral capital out of the false
doctrine of man's total depravity. They are engaged
in proving their sensibility by minute experience, in
discovering to what degree life is good and beauty
true and man teachable, and only when they have
served this apprenticeship to detail, and have
mastered a material multitude, will they be able to
capture once again and with more completeness and
certainty the ideals which moved with unargued
provocation the genius of their fathers.

5

Modern poetry, then, we may say in conclusion,
is, in spite of its lyrical bent, very closely, if unconsciously, related to modern morality and thought.
For the lyric in these days has moved far from its
origin in spontaneous song or its Victorian tendency
to relapse into decorative sentiment. Three circumstances in particular have dictated the modern
consciousness and hastened the reaction from a

weak æstheticism. Industrialism has instructed men in ugliness, science in a regard for fact, and war in the nakedness of pain. These influences in combination have impressed the modern poet with the need of pity, of caution and of truth. They have forced him to question vague and magnificent optimisms and to suspect the consolations of sentiment. Nature in the large, no less than formulas of virtue or religious dogmas, are come up to judgment, and life's value is sought not in a remote heaven, but in the heart and the will of the individual. Man in learning to defy the forces of nature and to distrust their sanctification in the deity of conventional religion, has discovered himself. Science has both enforced honesty and invited experiments. The poet no longer indulges in large gestures and splendid pomps. He observes the small things of life with a wistful scrutiny. He will neither escape from life into a world of purely sensational romance, nor drug his pain, his disgust or his anxiety with soothing narcotics. Rather he seeks to explore reality with a studious and, so far as he can, a disinterested vision, reconciling where possible what he desires with what is, but not shrinking from revealing the gulf which so often yawns between the ideal and the real. He has learnt that human life is a vicarious struggle by imperfect man towards the ideal, rather than an escape into a private paradise, and that art cannot therefore be compassed by superior people nor labelled by superior critics. The world, in fact, is a devastating spectacle, which only strength can face without disgust, and it is the omnipresent consciousness of this which explains that fusion of passion and irony, evident in some of the finest modern writers. Such an attitude can scarcely be avoided by men of feeling who are yet determined to show people what they are rather than what they might be.

That such an attitude entails too often a record of "unadjusted impressions," of moods rather than ideas, a lack too of coherency and power, and an occasional acceptance of insignificant realism, must be admitted. That the Freudian theory has also encouraged certain writers to sanctify unduly the unselected whims of the subconscious, is also apparent. But even in the excesses of modernism we read the symptoms of brave endeavour after a truer and finer freedom. Men are learning that the purpose of human life is not to deny either soul or sense, but to attain an equilibrium between them, between the brute in us and the God, the root and the branches soaring skyward. In this finely poised consciousness, spirit and flesh are positively wed and we experience reality to the full. The destructive and constructive forces, the positive and negative, the finite and infinite, the selfish and selfless do not make war on each other or merely balance each other in a pale and neutral compromise. They blend positively, creating out of their dualism a new unity, a new and varied splendour, as the white light blends with darkness into form and colour. The modern poet is often doubtless of smaller stature than the Victorian, but in his shocked refusal of the gilded lie, he is, we believe, more scrupulous of values, and beyond his own personal attainment, he is preparing surely for a time when the disintegrated elements of life may come together again in a new and deeper harmony, when a great poet may transcend the critical caution of these times and by a right and positive concentration of feeling, capture the suffrage of the world.

FINIS